Inspired Shakespeare

The Most Powerful Quotes From

Shakespeare's Plays

"Study is like the heaven's glorious sun."

Love's Labour's Lost, Act I Scene 1

THE PLAYS

INTRODUCTION

Shakespeare has delighted and inspired through the ages. His plays and poems deserve to be read, performed and quoted for as long as there are people to be moved by them.

This collection presents some of the most oft-cited quotations from Shakespeare's plays, along with many included for their intrinsic qualities.

The plays are arranged alphabetically with the quotes typically in order of appearance in the text. As this is a collection of quotations attributed to Shakespeare, and therefore a celebration of his genius, the texts are not included with attribution to particular characters. However, act and scene numbers are included with each quote if you would like to read more of the context surrounding the writing.

Enjoy this collection and we hope that you are able to use it to inspire yourself and others.

1.

ALL'S WELL THAT ENDS WELL

- Comedy -

Helen is in love with Bertram in a one-sided romance set in France and Italy.

"

It were all one,

That I should love a bright, particular star,

And think to wed it, he is so above me.

"

All's Well That Ends Well, Act I Scene 1

"

The hind, that would be mated by the lion,

Must die for love.

"

All's Well That Ends Well, Act I Scene 1

"

Our remedies oft in ourselves do lie,
Which we ascribe to Heaven.
"

All's Well That Ends Well, Act I Scene 1

"

Moderate lamentation is the right of the
dead, excessive grief the enemy to the living.
"

All's Well That Ends Well, Act I Scene 1

"

Love all, trust a few, do wrong to none.
"

All's Well That Ends Well, Act I Scene 1

"

His good remembrance, sir,
Lies richer in your thoughts than on his tomb
"

All's Well That Ends Well, Act I Scene 2

"

Service is no heritage.
"

All's Well That Ends Well, Act I Scene 3

"

If men could be contented to be what they
are, there were no fear in marriage
"

All's Well That Ends Well, Act I Scene 3

"

Even so it was with me when I was young.
If we are nature's, these are ours. This thorn
Doth to our rose of youth rightly belong.
Our blood to us, this to our blood is born:
It is the show and seal of nature's truth,
Where love's strong passion is impressed
in youth.
By our remembrances of days foregone,
Such were our faults, or then we thought
them none.

"

All's Well That Ends Well, Act I Scene 3

"Great floods have flown
From simple sources, and great seas have
dried
When miracles have by the great'st been
denied."

All's Well That Ends Well, Act II Scene 1

"

A young man married is a man that's
marred.

"

All's Well That Ends Well, Act II Scene 3

"

No legacy is so rich as honesty.

"

All's Well That Ends Well, Act II Scene 5

"

The web of our life is of a mingled yarn,
good and ill together.

"

All's Well That Ends Well, Act IV Scene 3

"

All's well that ends well, still the fine's the
crown;
Whate'er the course, the end is the renown.
"

All's Well That Ends Well, Act IV Scene 4

"

For we are old, and on our quick'st decrees
Th'inaudible and noiseless foot of time
Steals ere we can effect them.
"

All's Well That Ends Well, Act V Scene 3

"

Praising what is lost
Makes the remembrance dear.
"

All's Well That Ends Well, Act V Scene 3

"

'T is but the shadow of a wife you see,
The name and not the thing.
"

All's Well That Ends Well, Act V Scene 3

"

The bitter past, more welcome is the sweet.
"

All's Well That Ends Well, Act V Scene 3

2.

ANTONY AND CLEOPATRA

- Tragedy -

Mark Antony, a Roman leader, loves Cleopatra, the Queen of Egypt, but miscommunication threatens all.

"

There's beggary in the love that can be reckoned.

"

Antony and Cleopatra, Act I Scene 1

"

And you shall see in him
The triple pillar of the world transformed
Into a strumpet's fool.

"

Antony and Cleopatra, Act I Scene 1

"

Let Rome in Tiber melt, and the wide arch
Of the ranged empire fall: here is my space.
"

Antony and Cleopatra, Act I Scene 1

"

This grief is crowned with consolation.
"

Antony and Cleopatra, Act I Scene 2

"

Eternity was in our lips and eyes.
"

Antony and Cleopatra, Act I Scene 3

"

O happy horse, to bear the weight of Antony!
"

Antony and Cleopatra, Act I Scene 5

"

I was

A morsel for a monarch.
"

Antony and Cleopatra, Act I Scene 5

"

My salad days,

When I was green in judgment, cold in blood.
"

Antony and Cleopatra, Act I Scene 5

"

For her own person,
It beggared all description.

"

Antony and Cleopatra, Act II Scene 2

"

Age cannot wither her, nor custom stale
Her infinite variety; other women cloy
The appetites they feed; but she makes hungry
Where most she satisfies: for vilest things
Become themselves in her, that the holy priests
Bless her when she is riggish.

"

Antony and Cleopatra, Act II Scene 2

"

Egypt, thou knew'st too well
My heart was to thy rudder tied by th'strings
And thou shouldst tow me after.

"

Antony and Cleopatra, Act III Scene 11

"

I found you as a morsel cold upon
Dead Caesar's trencher.

"

Antony and Cleopatra, Act III Scene 13

"

O, wither'd is the garland of the war!
The soldier's pole is fall'n; young boys and girls
Are level now with men; the odds is gone,
And there is nothing left remarkable
Beneath the visiting moon.

"

Antony and Cleopatra, Act IV Scene 15

"

The breaking of so great a thing should make

A greater crack

"

Antony and Cleopatra, Act V Scene 1

"

Now boast thee, death, in thy possession lies

A lass unparalleled.

"

Antony and Cleopatra, Act V Scene 2

"She shall be buried by her Antony,

No grave upon the earth shall clip in it"

A pair so famous.

Antony and Cleopatra, Act V Scene 2

"

I have Immortal longings in me.

"

Antony and Cleopatra, Act V Scene 2

"

I am fire and air; my other elements
I give to baser life.

"

Antony and Cleopatra, Act V Scene 2

"

She shall be buried by her Antony:
No grave upon the earth shall clip in it
A pair so famous.

"

Antony and Cleopatra, Act V Scene 2

3.
AS YOU LIKE IT
- Comedy -

After escaping into the forest dressed as a shepherd, Rosalind finds Orlando, her love. He doesn't know it's her, giving Rosalind a chance to see if their love is true.

"

Well said: that was laid on with a trowel.

"

As You Like It, Act I Scene 2

"

My pride fell with my fortunes.

"

As You Like It, Act I Scene 2

"

Not a word?
Not one to throw at a dog.

"

As You Like It, Act I Scene 3

"

O how full of briers is this working day world!

"

As You Like It, Act I Scene 3

"

Sweet are the uses of adversity,
Which, like the toad, ugly and venomous,
Wears yet a precious jewel in his head;
And this our life, exempt from public haunt,
Finds tongues in trees, books in the running
brooks,
Sermons in stones, and good in every thing.
"

As You Like It, Act II Scene 1

"

"Poor deer," quoth he, "thou mak'st a
testament,
As wordlings do, giving thy sum of more
To that which had too much."
"

As You Like It, Act II Scene 1

"

And He that doth the ravens feed,
Yea, providently caters for the sparrow,
Be comfort to my age!

"

As You Like It, Act II Scene 3

"

For in my youth I never did apply
Hot and rebellious liquors in my blood,
Nor did not with unbashful forehead woo
The means of weakness and debility;
Therefore my age is as a lusty winter,
Frosty, but kindly: let me go with you;

"

As You Like It, Act II Scene 1

"
And railed on lady Fortune in good terms,
In good set terms....
And looking on it with lack-luster eye,
"Thus we may see," quoth he, "how the
world wags.
"

As You Like It, Act II Scene 7

"
And so, from hour to hour, we ripe and ripe,
And then, from hour to hour, we rot and rot;
And thereby hangs a tale.
"

As You Like It, Act II Scene 7

"
Motley's the only wear.
"

As You Like It, Act II Scene 7

"

If ladies be but young and fair,
They have the gift to know it.
"

As You Like It, Act II Scene 7

"

I must have liberty
Withal, as large a charter as the wind,
To blow on whom I please.
"

As You Like It, Act II Scene 7

"

The why is plain as way to parish church.
"

As You Like It, Act II Scene 7

"

All the world's a stage,
And all the men and women merely players;
They have their exits and their entrances,
And one man in his time plays many parts,
His acts being seven ages. At first the infant,
Mewling and puking in the nurse's arms.
Then, the whining school-boy with his satchel
And shining morning face, creeping like snail
Unwillingly to school. And then the lover,
Sighing like furnace, with a woeful ballad
Made to his mistress' eyebrow. Then, a soldier,
Full of strange oaths, and bearded like the pard,
Jealous in honour, sudden, and quick in quarrel,
Seeking the bubble reputation
Even in the cannon's mouth. And then, the
justice,
In fair round belly, with a good capon lined,
With eyes severe, and beard of formal cut,
Full of wise saws, and modern instances,
And so he plays his part. The sixth age shifts
Into the lean and slippered pantaloon,
With spectacles on nose and pouch on side,

His youthful hose, well saved, a world too wide
For his shrunk shank, and his big manly voice,
Turning again toward childish treble, pipes
And whistles in his sound. Last scene of all,
That ends this strange eventful history,
Is second childishness and mere oblivion,
Sans teeth, sans eyes, sans taste, sans everything.
"

As You Like It, Act II Scene 7, 'The Seven Ages of Man'

"

Blow, blow, thou winter wind,
Thou art not so unkind
As man's ingratitude.
"

As You Like It, Act II Scene 7

"

Hast any philosophy in thee, shepherd?
"

As You Like It, Act III Scene 2

"

Truly, I would the gods had made thee poetical.

"

As You Like It, Act III Scene 8

"

I had rather have a fool to make me merry, than experience to make me sad.

"

As You Like It, Act IV Scene 1

"

Men have died from time to time, and worms have eaten them, but not for love.

"

As You Like It, Act IV Scene 1

"

Pacing through the forest,
Chewing the food of sweet and bitter fancy.
"

As You Like It, Act IV Scene 3

"

How bitter a thing it is to look into happiness
through another man's eyes!
"

As You Like It, Act V Scene 2

"

Your If is the only peacemaker; much virtue
in If.
"

As You Like It, Act V Scene 4

"

Good wine needs no bush.

"

As You Like It, Epilogue

4.

COMEDY OF ERRORS

- Comedy -

After a shipwreck separates them from their twins,
Antipholus and his slave Dromio set out to find them.

"

I to the world am like a drop of water
That in the ocean seeks another drop,
Who, falling there to find his fellow forth,
Unseen, inquisitive, confounds himself.

"

Comedy of Errors, Act I Scene 2

"

Every why hath a wherefore.

"

Comedy of Errors, Act I Scene 2

"

Am I in earth, in heaven, or in hell?
Sleeping or waking, mad or well-advised?
"

Comedy of Errors, Act II Scene 2

"

Small cheer and great welcome makes a
merry feast.
"

Comedy of Errors, Act III Scene 1

"

O, villain, thou hast stol'n both mine office
and my name:
The one ne'er got me credit, the other mickle
blame.
"

Comedy of Errors, Act III Scene 1

"

If everyone knows us and we know none,
'Tis time, I think, to trudge, pack and be
gone.

"

Comedy of Errors, Act III Scene 2

"

He is deformed, crooked, old and sere,
Ill-faced, worse bodied, shapeless
everywhere,
Vicious, ungentle, foolish, blunt, unkind,
Stigmatical in making, worse in mind.

"

Comedy of Errors, Act IV Scene 2

"

Marry, he must have a long spoon that must
eat with the devil.
"

Comedy of Errors, Act IV Scene 3

"

They brought one Pinch, a hungry, lean-faced
villain,
A mere anatomy.
"

Comedy of Errors, Act V Scene 1

"

And now let's go hand in hand, not one
before another.
"

Comedy of Errors, Act V Scene 1

5.

CORIOLANUS

- Tragedy -

*A military leader is banished from Rome and later
returns to attack his own city.*

"

Had I a dozen sons, each in my love alike,
and none less dear than thine and my good
Marcius, I had rather had eleven die nobly
for their country than one voluptuously
surfeit out of action.

"

Coriolanus, Act I Scene 3

"

If any think brave death outweighs bad life,

And that his country's dearer than himself,

Let him alone, or so many so minded,

Wave thus to express his disposition
"

Coriolanus, Act I Scene 6

"

Nature teaches beasts to know their friends.
"

Coriolanus, Act II Scene 1

"

More of your conversation would infect my
brain, being the herdsmen of the beastly
plebeians.
"

Coriolanus, Act II Scene 1

"

What is the city but the people?
"

Coriolanus, Act II Scene 1

"

But now 'tis odds beyond arithmetic,
And manhood is called foolery when it
stands
Against a falling fabric.
"

Coriolanus, Act III Scene 1

"

His nature is too noble for the world:
He would not flatter Neptune for his trident,
Or Jove for's power to thunder.
"

Coriolanus, Act III Scene 1

"

Action is eloquence.

"

Coriolanus, Act III Scene 2

"

There is a world elsewhere.

"

Coriolanus, Act III Scene 3

"

Anger's my meat: I sup upon myself,
And so shall starve with feeding.

"

Coriolanus, Act IV Scene 2

"

Let me have war, say I: it exceeds peace as far
as day does night: it's sprightly waking,
audible, and full of vent. Peace is a very
apoplexy, lethargy; mulled, deaf, sleepy,
insensible: a getter of more bastard children
than war's a destroyer of men.

"

Coriolanus, Act IV Scene 5

"

If you have writ your annals true, 't is there,
That, like an eagle in a dovecote, I
Fluttered your Volscians in Corioles.
Alone I did it. Boy!

"

Coriolanus, Act V Scene 6

"

My rage is gone,
And I am struck with sorrow.

"

Coriolanus, Act V Scene 6

6.

CYMBELINE

- Tragedy -

The British King Cymbeline banishes his daughter Innogen's husband while Innogen is accused of being unfaithful.

"

Lest the bargain should catch cold and starve.

"

Cymbeline, Act I Scene 4

"

Boldness be my friend:
Arm me audacity from head to foot!

"

Cymbeline, Act I Scene 6

"

Every jack-slave hath his bellyful of fighting.
"

Cymbeline, Act II Scene 1

"

How bravely thou becom'st thy bed!
"

Cymbeline, Act II Scene 2

"

Ambitions, covetings, change of prides, disdain,
Nice longing, slanders, mutability,
All faults that may be named, nay, that hell knows,
Why, hers, in part of all.
"

Cymbeline, Act II Scene 4

"

His fortunes all lie speechless, and his name
Is at last gasp.
"

Cymbeline, Act I Scene 5

"

Boldness be my friend!
Arm me, audacity, from head to foot!
"

Cymbeline, Act I Scene 6

"

Hark! hark! the lark at heaven's gate sings
"

Cymbeline, Act II Scene 3

"

Some griefs are med'cinable.
"

Cymbeline, Act III Scene 2

"

Our cage
We make a choir, as doth the prisoned bird,
And sing our bondage freely.
"

Cymbeline, Act III Scene 3

"

The game is up.
"

Cymbeline, Act III Scene 3

"

'Tis slander,

Whose edge is sharper than the sword, whose tongue

Outvenoms all the worms of Nile, whose breath

Rides on the posting winds, and doth belie

All corners of the world.

"

Cymbeline, Act III Scene 4

"

I have not slept one wink.

"

Cymbeline, Act III Scene 4

"

Weariness

Can snore upon the flint, when restive sloth

Finds the down pillow hard.

"

Cymbeline, Act III Scene 6"

I see a man's life is a tedious one.

"

Cymbeline, Act III Scene 6

"

All gold and silver rather turn to dirt.

"

Cymbeline, Act III Scene 6

"

Play judge and executioner all himself.

"

Cymbeline, Act IV Scene 2

"

Fear no more the heat o' the sun,
Nor the furious winter's rages,
Thou thy worldly task hast done,
Home art gone, and ta'en thy wages.
Golden lads and girls all must,
As chimney-sweepers, come to dust.

"

Cymbeline, Act IV Scene 2

"

Hang there like fruit, my soul,
Till the tree die.

"

Cymbeline, Act V Scene 4

"

O, never say hereafter

But I am truest speaker: you call'd me
brother

When I was but your sister; I you, brothers,

When you were so indeed.

"

Cymbeline, Act V Scene 5

7.

HAMLET

- Tragedy -

The ghost of the King of Denmark tells his son Hamlet to avenge his murder.

"

This bodes some strange eruption to our state.

"

Hamlet, Act I Scene 1

"

In the most high and palmy state of Rome,
A little ere the mightiest Julius fell,
The graves stood tenantless, and the sheeted
dead
Did squeak and gibber in the Roman streets.
"

Hamlet, Act I Scene 1

"

And then it started like a guilty thing
Upon a fearful summons.
"

Hamlet, Act I Scene 1

"

Some say, that ever 'gainst that season comes

Wherein our Saviour's birth is celebrated,

This bird of dawning singeth all night long.

And then they say no spirit dares stir abroad,

The nights are wholesome; then no planets strike,

No fairy takes, nor witch hath power to charm,

So hallowed and so gracious is the time.
"

Hamlet, Act I Scene 1

"

The head is not more native to the heart.
"

Hamlet, Act I Scene 2

"

A little more than kin, and less than kind.
"

Hamlet, Act I Scene 2

"

Seems, madam! Nay, it is; I know not 'seems.'
"

Hamlet, Act I Scene 2

"

But I have that within which passeth show;
These, but the trappings and the suits of woe.
"

Hamlet, Act I Scene 2

"

O that this too, too solid flesh would melt,

Thaw, and resolve itself into a dew!

Or that the Everlasting had not fixed

His canon 'gainst self-slaughter! O God! O God!

How weary, stale, flat, and unprofitable

Seem to me all the uses of this world!

"

Hamlet, Act I Scene 2

"

O, that this too too solid flesh would melt

Thaw and resolve itself into a dew!

Or that the Everlasting had not fix'd

His canon 'gainst self-slaughter! O God! God!

How weary, stale, flat and unprofitable,

Seem to me all the uses of this world!

Fie on't! ah fie! 'tis an unweeded garden,

That grows to seed; things rank and gross in nature

Possess it merely. That it should come to this!

But two months dead: nay, not so much, not two:

So excellent a king; that was, to this,

Hyperion to a satyr; so loving to my mother

That he might not beteem the winds of heaven

Visit her face too roughly. Heaven and earth!

Must I remember? why, she would hang on him,

As if increase of appetite had grown

By what it fed on: and yet, within a month–

Let me not think on't–Frailty, thy name is woman!–

A little month, or ere those shoes were old

With which she follow'd my poor father's body,

Like Niobe, all tears:–why she, even she–

O, God! a beast, that wants discourse of reason,

Would have mourn'd longer–married with my uncle,

My father's brother, but no more like my father

Than I to Hercules: within a month:

Ere yet the salt of most unrighteous tears

Had left the flushing in her galled eyes,

She married. O, most wicked speed, to post

With such dexterity to incestuous sheets!

It is not nor it cannot come to good:

But break, my heart; for I must hold my tongue.

"

Hamlet, Act I Scene 2

"

Thrift, thrift, Horatio! the funeral baked meats
Did coldly furnish forth the marriage tables.
"

Hamlet, Act I Scene 2

"

In my mind's eye, Horatio.
"

Hamlet, Act I Scene 2

"

He was a man, take him for all in all,
I shall not look upon his like again.
"

Hamlet, Act I Scene 2

"

A countenance more
In sorrow than in anger.
"

Hamlet, Act I Scene 2

"

And in the morn and liquid dew of youth.
"

Hamlet, Act I Scene 3

"

Give thy thoughts no tongue,
Nor any unproportion'd thought his act.
Be thou familiar, but by no means vulgar.
Those friends thou hast, and their adoption
tried,
Grapple them unto thy soul with hoops of steel;
But do not dull thy palm with entertainment

Of each new-hatch'd, unfledg'd comrade. Beware
Of entrance to a quarrel; but, being in,
Bear't that the opposed may beware of thee.
Give every man thine ear, but few thy voice:
Take each man's censure, but reserve thy
judgment.
Costly thy habit as thy purse can buy,
But not express'd in fancy; rich, not gaudy:
For the apparel oft proclaims the man;
And they in France of the best rank and station
Are most select and generous chief in that.
Neither a borrower nor a lender be:
For loan oft loses both itself and friend;
And borrowing dulls the edge of husbandry.
This above all, — to thine own self be true;
And it must follow, as the night the day,
Thou canst not then be false to any man.
"

Hamlet, Act I Scene 3

"

Springes to catch woodcocks.
"

Hamlet, Act I Scene 3

"

But to my mind—though I am native here,
And to the manner born—it is a custom
More honored in the breach than the
observance.
"

Hamlet, Act I Scene 4

"

Angels and ministers of grace, defend us!
"

Hamlet, Act I Scene 4

"

Thou com'st in such a questionable shape,
That I will speak to thee.
"

Hamlet, Act I Scene 4

"

Let me not burst in ignorance!
"

Hamlet, Act I Scene 4

"

I do not set my life at a pin's fee.
"

Hamlet, Act I Scene 4

"

Something is rotten in the state of Denmark.
"

Hamlet, Act I Scene 4

"

I could a tale unfold, whose lightest word
Would harrow up thy soul; freeze thy young
blood;
Make thy two eyes, like stars, start from their
spheres;
Thy knotted and combined locks to part,
And each particular hair to stand on end,
Like quills upon the fretful Porcupine.
"

Hamlet, Act I Scene 5

"

O my prophetic soul! my uncle!
"

Hamlet, Act I Scene 5

"

O Hamlet, what a falling-off was there!

"

Hamlet, Act I Scene 5

"

No reckoning made, but sent to my account
With all my imperfections on my head.

"

Hamlet, Act I Scene 5

"

The glowworm shows the matin to be near
And 'gins to pale his uneffectual fire.

"

Hamlet, Act I Scene 5

"

There needs no ghost, my lord, come from
the grave,
To tell us this.
"

Hamlet, Act I Scene 5

"

There are more things in heaven and earth,
Horatio,
Than are dreamt of in your philosophy.
"

Hamlet, Act I Scene 5

"

The time is out of joint.
"

Hamlet, Act I Scene 5

"

This is the very ecstasy of love.
"

Hamlet, Act II Scene 1

"

Brevity is the soul of wit.
"

Hamlet, Act II Scene 2

"

That he is mad, 'tis true; 'tis true, 'tis pity;
And pity 'tis, 'tis true.
"

Hamlet, Act II Scene 2

"

Doubt thou the stars are tire;
Doubt that the sun doth move;
Doubt truth to be a liar;
But never doubt I love.
"

Hamlet, Act II Scene 2

"

Still harping on my daughter.
"

Hamlet, Act II Scene 2

"

Though this be madness, yet there's method
in it.
"

Hamlet, Act II Scene 2

"

What a piece of work is man! How noble in reason! how infinite in faculties! in form and moving, how express and admirable! in action, how like an angel! in apprehension, how like a God!

"

Hamlet, Act II Scene 2

"

Man delights not me—nor woman neither.

"

Hamlet, Act II Scene 2

"

I know a hawk from a hand-saw.

"

Hamlet, Act II Scene 2

"

Come, give us a taste of your quality.
"

Hamlet, Act II Scene 2

"

'Twas caviare to the general.
"

Hamlet, Act II Scene 2

"

What's Hecuba to him, or he to Hecuba?
"

Hamlet, Act II Scene 2

"

The play's the thing,
Wherein I'll catch the conscience of the king.
"

Hamlet, Act II Scene 2

"

We are oft to blame in this, —
'Tis too much prov'd, — that with devotion's
visage,
And pious action, we do sugar o'er
The devil himself.

"

Hamlet, Act III Scene 1

"

To be, or not to be? that is the question:
Whether 'tis nobler in the mind, to suffer
The slings and arrows of outrageous fortune,
Or to take arms against a sea of troubles,
And, by opposing, end them?—To die—to
sleep—
No more—and, by a sleep, to say we end
The heartache, and the thousand natural
shocks
That flesh is heir to—'tis a consummation
Devoutly to be wished. To die—to sleep—

To sleep! perchance, to dream—ay, there's
the rub;
For in that sleep of death what dreams may
come,
When we have shuffled off this mortal coil,
Must give us pause.
The spurns
That patient merit of the unworthy takes;
When he himself might his quietus make
With a bare bodkin. Who would fardels bear,
To grunt and sweat under a weary life,
But that the dread of something after death—
The undiscovered country, from whose
bourne
No traveler returns—puzzles the will,
And makes us rather bear those ills we have,
Than fly to others that we know not of?
Thus conscience does make cowards of us all,
And thus the native hue of resolution
Is sicklied o'er with the pale cast of thought.
Nymph, in thy orisons

Be all my sins remembered.

"

Hamlet, Act III Scene 1

"

Be thou as chaste as ice, as pure as snow,
thon shalt not escape calumny.

"

Hamlet, Act III Scene 1

"

The glass of fashion, and the mould of form,
The observed of all observers!

"

Hamlet, Act III Scene 1

"

It out-herods Herod. Pray you, avoid it.

"

Hamlet, Act III Scene 2

"

Suit the action to the word, the word to the action.

"

Hamlet, Act III Scene 2

"

To hold, as 'twere, the mirror up to nature.

"

Hamlet, Act III Scene 2

"

I have thought some of nature's journeymen
had made men, and not made them well,
they imitated humanity so abominably.

"

Hamlet, Act III Scene 2

"

No, let the candied tongue lick absurd pomp;
And crook the pregnant hinges of the knee,
Where thrift may follow fawning.

"

Hamlet, Act III Scene 2

"

Give me that man

That is not passion's slave, and I will wear

him

In my heart's core, ay, in my heart of hearts,

As I do thee.

"

Hamlet, Act III Scene 2

"

Something too much of this.

"

Hamlet, Act III Scene 2

"

Here's metal more attractive.

"

Hamlet, Act III Scene 2

"

The lady doth protest too much, methinks.

"

Hamlet, Act III Scene 2

"

Let the galled jade wince, our withers are un-

wrung.

"

Hamlet, Act III Scene 2

"

Why, let the strucken deer go weep,

The hart ungalled play;

For some must watch, while some must

sleep;

Thus runs the world away.

"

Hamlet, Act III Scene 2

"

It will discourse most eloquent music.

"

Hamlet, Act III Scene 2

"

Very like a whale.

"

Hamlet, Act III Scene 2

"

They fool me to the top of my bent.

"

Hamlet, Act III Scene 2

"

'Tis now the very witching time of night,
When churchyards yawn, and hell itself
breathes out
Contagion to this world.
"

Hamlet, Act III Scene 2

"

O my offence is rank, it smells to heaven.
"

Hamlet, Act III Scene 3

"

Look here, upon this picture, and on this;
The counterfeit presentment of two brothers.
See what a grace was seated on this brow!
Hyperion's curls; the front of Jove himself;
An eye like Mars, to threaten and command.
A combination, and a form, indeed,
Where every god did seem to set his seal,
To give the world assurance of a man.
"

Hamlet, Act III Scene 4

"

A king of shreds and patches.
"

Hamlet, Act III Scene 4

"

This is the very coinage of your brain.
"

Hamlet, Act III Scene 4

"

Lay not that flattering unction to your soul.
"

Hamlet, Act III Scene 4

"

Assume a virtue, if you have it not.
"

Hamlet, Act III Scene 4

"

For 'tis the sport to have the engineer
Hoist with his own petard.
"

Hamlet, Act III Scene 4

"

When sorrows come, they come not single spies,
But in battalions!

"

Hamlet, Act IV Scene 5

"

There's such divinity doth hedge a king,
That treason can but peep to what it would.

"

Hamlet, Act IV Scene 5

"

How absolute the knave is! we must speak by the card, or equivocation will undo us.

"

Hamlet, Act V Scene 1

"

Alas, poor Yorick! I knew him, Horatio: a fellow of infinite jest; of most excellent fancy.
"

Hamlet, Act V Scene 1

"

Where be your gibes now? your gambols? your songs? your flashes of merriment, that were wont to set the table on a roar?
"

Hamlet, Act V Scene 1

"

To what base uses we may return, Horatio!
"

Hamlet, Act V Scene 1

"

Imperial Caesar, dead, and turned to clay,
Might stop a hole to keep the wind away.
"

Hamlet, Act V Scene 1

"

Sir, though I am not splenetive and rash,
Yet have I in me something dangerous.
"

Hamlet, Act V Scene 1

"

The cat will mew, and dog will have his day.
"

Hamlet, Act V Scene 1

"

There's a divinity that shapes our ends,
Rough-hew them how we will.
"

Hamlet, Act V Scene 2

"

There is a special providence in the fall of a
sparrow.
"

Hamlet, Act V Scene 2

"

A hit, a very palpable hit.
"

Hamlet, Act V Scene 2

"

Now cracks a noble heart. Good-night, sweet
prince;
And flights of angels sing thee to thy rest.
"

Hamlet, Act V Scene 2

"

The sight is dismal;
And our affairs from England come too late:
The ears are senseless that should give us
hearing,
To tell him his commandment is fulfill'd,
That Rosencrantz and Guildenstern are dead:
Where should we have our thanks?
"

Hamlet, Act V Scene 2

"

Bear Hamlet, like a soldier, to the stage.
"

Hamlet, Act V Scene 2

"

Go, bid the soldiers shoot.
"

Hamlet, Act V Scene 2

8.

HENRY IV PART I

- History -

After an argument, a battle ensues between King Henry IV and Hotspur.

"

'Tis my vocation, Hal; 'tis no sin for a man to labor in his vocation.

"

Henry IV Part I, Act I Scene 2

"

He will give the devil his due.

"

Henry IV Part I, Act I Scene 2

"

And, as the soldiers bore dead bodies by,
He called them untaught knaves,
unmannerly,
To bring a slovenly, unhandsome corse
Betwixt the wind and his nobility.
"

Henry IV Part I, Act I Scene 3

"

By heaven, methinks it were an easy leap,
To pluck bright honor from the pale-faced
moon."

Henry IV Part I, Act I Scene 3

"

I know a trick worth two of that.
"

Henry IV Part I, Act II Scene 1

"

Call you that backing of your friends? a
plague upon such backing!

"

Henry IV Part I, Act II Scene 4

"

A plague of sighing and grief! it blows a man
up like a bladder.

"

Henry IV Part I, Act II Scene 4

"

Give you a reason on compulsion! if reasons
were as plenty as blackberries, I would give
no man a reason upon compulsion.

"

Henry IV Part I, Act II Scene 4

"

I was a coward on instinct.

"

Henry IV Part I, Act II Scene 4

"

No more of that, Hal, an thou lovest me.

"

Henry IV Part I, Act II Scene 4

"

Glen. I can call spirits from the vasty deep.
Hot. Why, so can I, or so can any man: But
will they come when you do call for them?

"

Henry IV Part I, Act III Scene 1

"

Tell truth and shame the devil.

"

Henry IV Part I, Act III Scene 1

"

I had rather be a kitten, and cry mew,
Than one of these same meter ballad-
mongers.

"

Henry IV Part I, Act III Scene 1

"

Shall I not take mine ease in mine inn?

"

Henry IV Part I, Act III Scene 3

"

I could have better spared a better man.
"

Henry IV Part I, Act V Scene 4

"

The better part of valor is—discretion.
"

Henry IV Part I, Act V Scene 4

"

Lord, Lord, how this world is given to lying!
I grant you, I was down, and out of breath;
and so was he: but we rose both at an instant,
and fought a long hour by Shrewsbury clock.
"

Henry IV Part I, Act V Scene 4

9.

HENRY IV PART II

- History -

Prince Hal prepares to be king while his father suffers from illness.

"

Rumour is a pipe
Blown by surmises, jealousies, conjectures
And of so easy and so plain a stop
That the blunt monster with uncounted heads,
The still-discordant wavering multitude,
Can play upon it.
"

Henry IV Part II, Prologue

"

Even such a man, so faint, so spiritless.
So dull, so dead in look, so woebegone,
Drew Priam's curtain in the dead of night,
And would have told him, half his Troy was
burned.
"

Henry IV Part II, Act I Scene 1

"

Yet the first bringer of unwelcome news
Hath but a losing office; and his tongue
Sounds ever after as a sullen bell,
Remembered knolling a departed friend.
"

Henry IV Part II, Act I Scene 1

"

I am not only witty in myself, but the cause that wit is in other men.

"

Henry IV Part II, Act I Scene 2

"

He hath eaten me out of house and home.

"

Henry IV Part II, Act I I Scene 2

"

He was, indeed, the glass
Wherein the noble youth did dress themselves.

"

Henry IV Part II, Act I I Scene 3

"

Sleep, gentle sleep,

Nature's soft nurse, how have I frighted thee,

That thou no more wilt weigh my eyelids

down,

And steep my senses in forgetfulness?

"

Henry IV Part II, Act III Scene 1

"

With all appliances and means to boot.

"

Henry IV Part II, Act III Scene 1

"

Uneasy lies the head that wears a crown.

"

Henry IV Part II, Act III Scene 1

"

He hath a tear for pity, and a hand
Open as day for melting charity.
"

Henry IV Part II, Act IV Scene 4

"

Thy wish was father, Harry, to that thought:
I stay too long by thee, I weary thee.
Dost thou so hunger for mine empty chair
That thou wilt needs invest thee with my honours
Before thy hour be ripe? O foolish youth!
"

Henry IV Part II, Act IV Scene 5

"

His cares are now all ended.
"

Henry IV Part II, Act V Scene 2

"

Under which king, Bezonian? Speak, or die.
"

Henry IV Part II, Act V Scene 3

"

How ill white hairs become a fool and jester!
"

Henry IV Part II, Act V Scene 5

10.
HENRY V
- History -

Covering the events around the Battle of Agincourt, this play sees King Henry V at war with France and in love with a princess of that country.

"

O, for a muse of fire, that would ascend
The brightest heaven of invention,
A kingdom for a stage, princes to act
And monarchs to behold the swelling scene!

"

Henry V, Prologue

"

Consideration like an angel came,
And whipped the offending Adam out of
him.
"

Henry V, Act I Scene 1

"

When he speaks,
The air, a chartered libertine, is still.
"

Henry V, Act I Scene 1

"

Base is the slave that pays.
"

Henry V, Act II Scene 1

"

His nose was as sharp as a pen,
and a' babbled of green fields.
"

Henry V, Act II Scene 3

"

Once more unto the breach, dear friends,
once more,
Or close the wall up with our English dead.
"

Henry V, Act III Scene 1

"

With busy hammers closing rivets up,
Give dreadful note of preparation.
"

Henry V, Act IV Chorus

"

This story shall the good man teach his son,

And Crispin Crispian shall ne'er go by,

From this day to the ending of the world,

But we in it shall be remembered;

We few, we happy few, we band of brothers.

For he to-day that sheds his blood with me

Shall be my brother.
"

Henry V, Act IV Scene 3

"

Then shall our names,

Familiar in their mouths as household words

—

Harry the King, Bedford and Exeter,

Warwick and Talbot, Salisbury and Gloster

—

Be in their flowing cups freshly remembered.
"

Henry V, Act IV Scene 3

"

There is occasions and causes why and
wherefore in all things.

"

Henry V, Act V Scene 1

"

A good heart, Kate, is the sun and the moon
— or rather the sun and not the moon, for it
shines bright and never changes, but keeps
his course truly. If thou would have such a
one, take me: and take me, take a soldier:
take a soldier, take a king.

"

Henry V, Act V Scene 2

"

Dear Kate, you and I cannot be confined
within the weak list of a country's fashion:
we are the makers of manners, Kate.

"

Henry V, Act V Scene 2

11.
HENRY VI PART I
- History -

Henry VI becomes king while his noble houses squabble with each other instead of focusing on new threats from France.

"

My thoughts are whirled like a potter's wheel:
I know not where I am, nor what I do.

"

Henry VI Part I, Act I Scene 5

"

I have heard it said, unbidden guests
Are often welcomest when they are gone.

"

Henry VI Part I, Act 2 Scene 2

"

Faith, I have been a truant in the law,
And never yet could frame my will to it,
And therefore frame the law unto my will.

"

Henry VI Part I, Act II Scene 4

"

I have perhaps some shallow spirit of
judgement:
But in these nice sharp quillets of the law,
Good faith, I am no wiser than a daw.

"

Henry VI Part I, Act II Scene 4

"

Here I prophesy: this brawl today,
Grown to this faction in the Temple garden,
Shall send, between the red rose and the
white,
A thousand souls to death and deadly night.
"

Henry VI Part I, Act II Scene 4

"

Defer no time, delays have dangerous ends.
"

Henry VI Part I, Act III Scene 2

"

No simple man that sees
This jarring discord of nobility,
This shouldering of each other in the court,
This factious bandying of their favourites,
But that it doth presage some ill event.
"

Henry VI Part I, Act IV Scene 1

"

I owe him little duty, and less love.
"

Henry VI Part I, Act IV Scene 1

"

Here on my knee I beg mortality,
Rather than life preserved with infamy.
"

Henry VI Part I, Act IV Scene 5

"

So doth the swan her downy cygnets save,
Keeping them prisoners underneath her
wings.

"

Henry VI Part I, Act V Scene 3

"

She's beautiful; and therefore to be wooed:
She is a woman; therefore to be won.

"

Henry VI Part I, Act V Scene 3

"

To be a queen in bondage is more vile
Than is a slave in base servility.

"

Henry VI Part I, Act V Scene 3

"

Marriage is a matter of more worth
Than to be dealt in by attorneyship.

"

Henry VI Part I, Act V Scene 5

12.

HENRY VI PART II

- History -

King Henry VI marries against the wishes of his nobles while plots are made against him from all sides.

"

Could I come near your beauty with my nails,

I'd set my ten commandments in your face.

"

Henry VI Part II, Act I Scene 3

"

How irksome is this music to my heart!

When such strings jar, what hope of harmony?

"

Henry VI Part II, Act II Scene 1

"

Smooth runs the water where the brook is
deep:
And in his simple show he harbours treason.
"

Henry VI Part II, Act III Scene 1

"

The fox barks not when he would steal the
lamb.
"

Henry VI Part II, Act III Scene 1

"

The commons, like an angry hive of bees
That want their leader, scatter up and down
And care not who they sting in his revenge.
"

Henry VI Part II, Act III Scene 2

"

For where thou art, there is the world itself,
With every several pleasure in the world:
And where thou art not, desolation.
"

Henry VI Part II, Act III Scene 2

"

Small things make base men proud.
"

Henry VI Part II, Act IV Scene 1

"

True nobility is exempt from fear.
"

Henry VI Part II, Act IV Scene 1

"

The first thing we do, let's kill all the lawyers.

"

Henry VI Part II, Act IV Scene 2

"

Is not this a lamentable thing, that of the skin of an innocent lamb should be made parchment? That parchment, being scribbled o'er, should undo a man?

"

Henry VI Part II, Act IV Scene 2

"

Thou hast most traitorously corrupted the youth of the realm in erecting a grammar school.

"

Henry VI Part II, Act IV Scene 7

"

And seeing ignorance is the curse of God,
Knowledge the wing wherewith we fly to
heaven.

"

Henry VI Part II, Act IV Scene 7

"

It is great sin, to swear unto a sin;
But greater sin, to keep a sinful oath.

"

Henry VI Part II, Act V Scene 1

"

Can we outrun the heavens?

"

Henry VI Part II, Act V Scene 2

13.
HENRY VI PART III
- History -

King Henry VI faces war, exile and imprisonment in the turbulent final stages of his life.

"

I am your butt, and I abide your shot.

"

Henry VI Part III, Act I Scene 1

"

Farewell, faint-hearted and degenerate king, In whose cold blood no spark of honour bides.

"

Henry VI Part III, Act I Scene 1

"

How sweet a thing it is to wear a crown,
Within whose circuit is Elysium
And all that poets feign of bliss and joy.
"

Henry VI Part III, Act I Scene 2

"

O, tiger's heart wrapt in a woman's hide!
"

Henry VI Part III, Act I Scene 4

"

Women are soft, mild, pitiful and flexible,
Thou stern, obdurate, flinty, rough,
remorseless.
"

Henry VI Part III, Act I Scene 4

"

To weep is to make less the depth of grief:
Tears then for babes; blows and revenge for
me.
"

Henry VI Part III, Act II Scene 1

"

The smallest worm will turn being trodden
on."

Henry VI Part III, Act II Scene 2

"

O God! Methinks it were a happy life,
To be no better than a homely swain,
To sit upon a hill, as I do now,
To carve out dials quaintly, point by point,
Thereby to see the minutes how they run:
"

Henry VI Part III, Act II Scene 5

"

Let me embrace the sour adversaries
For wise men say it is the wisest course.
"

Henry VI Part III, Act III Scene 1

"

My crown is in my heart, not on my head.
"

Henry VI Part III, Act III Scene 1

"

Yet hasty marriage seldom proveth well.

"

Henry VI Part III, Act IV Scene 1

"

For trust not him that hath once broken faith.

"

Henry VI Part III, Act IV Scene 4

"

Fearless minds climb soonest unto crowns.

"

Henry VI Part III, Act IV Scene 7

"

And live we how we can, yet die we must.

"

Henry VI Part III, Act V Scene 2

"

Suspicion always haunts the guilty mind;
The thief doth fear each bush an officer.
"

Henry VI Part III, Act V Scene 6

14.
HENRY VIII
- History -

King Henry VIII grants too much power to Cardinal Wolsey while he divorces his wife Katharine and marries Anne Boleyn.

"

Order gave each thing view.
"

Henry VIII, Act I Scene 1

"

No man's pie is freed
From his ambitious finger.
"

Henry VIII, Act I Scene 1

"

Anger is like
A full-hot horse, who being allow'd his way,
Self-mettle tires him.
"

Henry VIII, Act I Scene 1

"

Be to yourself
As you would to your friend.
"

Henry VIII, Act I Scene 1

"

Heat not a furnace for your foe so hot
That it do singe yourself.
"

Henry VIII, Act I Scene 1

"

'Tis but the fate of place, and the rough brake
That virtue must go through.
"

Henry VIII, Act I Scene 2

"

The mirror of all courtesy.
"

Henry VIII, Act II Scene 1

"

'Tis better to be lowly born,
And range with humble livers in content,
Than to be perked up in a glist'ring grief,
And wear a golden sorrow.
"

Henry VIII, Act II Scene 3

"

Orpheus, with his lute made trees,
And the mountain tops that freeze,
Bow themselves when he did sing.
"

Henry VIII, Act III Scene 1

"

I have touched the highest point of all my
greatness,
And from that full meridian of my glory,
I haste now to my setting. I shall fall
Like a bright exhalation in the evening,
And no man see me more.
"

Henry VIII, Act III Scene 2

"

I feel within me
A peace above all earthly dignities,
A still and quiet conscience.
"

Henry VIII, Act III Scene 2

"

And then to breakfast with
What appetite you have.
"

Henry VIII, Act III Scene 2

"

A load would sink a navy: too much honour.
"

Henry VIII, Act III Scene 2

"

Love thyself last: cherish those hearts that
hate thee:
Corruption wins not more than honesty.

"

Henry VIII, Act III Scene 2

"

Men's evil manners live in brass, their virtues
We write in water.

"

Henry VIII, Act IV Scene 2

"

Those about her
From her shall read the perfect ways of
honour.

"

Henry VIII, Act V Scene 4

15.

JULIUS CAESAR

- Tragedy -

Julius Caesar is the victim of a plot hatched by conspirators including his friend Brutus.

"

Beware the Ides of March.

"

Julius Caesar, Act I Scene 2

"

And it is very much lamented, Brutus, That you have no such mirrors as will turn Your hidden worthiness into your eye.

"

Julius Caesar, Act I Scene 2

"

Into what dangers would you lead me,
Cassius,
That you would have me seek into myself
For that which is not in me?
"

Julius Caesar, Act I Scene 2

"

Men at some time are masters of their fates.
The fault, dear Brutus, is not in our stars
But in ourselves, that we are underlings.
"

Julius Caesar, Act I Scene 2

"

I cannot tell what you and other men
Think of this life; but for my single self,
I had as lief not be as live to be
In awe of such a thing as I myself.
"

Julius Caesar, Act I Scene 2

"

Dar'st thou, Cassius, now
Leap in with me into this angry flood,
And swim to yonder point?—Upon the
word,
Accoutred as I was, I plunged in,
And bade him follow.
"

Julius Caesar, Act I Scene 2

"

Ye gods, it doth amaze me,
A man of such a feeble temper should
So get the start of the majestic world,
And bear the palm alone.
"

Julius Caesar, Act I Scene 2

"

Why, man, he doth bestride the narrow
world,
Like a Colossus, and we petty men
Walk under his huge legs, and peep about
To find ourselves dishonorable graves.
"

Julius Caesar, Act I Scene 2

"

Let me have men about me that are fat;
Sleek-headed men, and such as sleep o'
nights;
Yond' Cassius has a lean and hungry look;
He thinks too much: such men are
dangerous.
"

Julius Caesar, Act I Scene 2

"

Seldom he smiles; and smiles in such a sort,
As if he mocked himself, and scorned his
spirit,
That could be moved to smile at anything.
"

Julius Caesar, Act I Scene 2

"

But, for mine own part, it was Greek to me.

"

Julius Caesar, Act I Scene 2

"

Between the acting of a dreadful thing
And the first motion, all the interim is
Like a phantasma, or a hideous dream.

"

Julius Caesar, Act I Scene 2

"

Yon are my true and honorable wife,
As dear to me as the ruddy drops
That visit my sad heart.

"

Julius Caesar, Act II Scene 1

"

Cowards die many times before their deaths;
The valiant never taste of death but once.
"

Julius Caesar, Act II Scene 2

"

Though last, not least, in love.
"

Julius Caesar, Act III Scene 1

"

Cry Havoc, and let slip the dogs of war.
"

Julius Caesar, Act III Scene 1

"

Romans, countrymen, and lovers! hear me
for my cause; and be silent that you may
hear.

"

Julius Caesar, Act III Scene 2

"

Not that I loved Caesar less, but that I loved
Rome more.

"

Julius Caesar, Act III Scene 2

"

Who is here so base, that would be a
bondman? If any, speak: for him have I
offended.

"

Julius Caesar, Act III Scene 2

"

The evil that men do lives after them;
The good is oft interred with their bones.
"

Julius Caesar, Act III Scene 2

"

For Brutus is an honorable man;
So are they all, all honorable men.
"

Julius Caesar, Act III Scene 2

"

When that the poor have cried, Caesar hath
wept;
Ambition should be made of sterner stuff.
"

Julius Caesar, Act III Scene 2

"

But yesterday, the word of Caesar might
Have stood against the world; now lies he
there,
And none so poor to do him reverence.
"

Julius Caesar, Act III Scene 2

"

If you have years, prepare to shed them now.
"

Julius Caesar, Act III Scene 2

"

See, what a rent the envious Casca made!
"

Julius Caesar, Act III Scene 2

"

This was the most unkindest cut of all.
"

Julius Caesar, Act III Scene 2

"

Great Caesar fell.
O what a fall was there, my countrymen!
"

Julius Caesar, Act III Scene 2

"

Put a tongue
In every wound of Caesar, that should move
The stones of Borne to rise and mutiny.
"

Julius Caesar, Act III Scene 2

"

There are no tricks in plain and simple faith.
"

Julius Caesar, Act IV Scene 2

"

I had rather be a dog, and bay the moon,
Than such a Roman.
"

Julius Caesar, Act IV Scene 3

"

There is no terror, Cassius, in your threats
For I am armed so strong in honesty,
That they pass by me as the idle wind,
Which I respect not.
"

Julius Caesar, Act IV Scene 3

"

A friend should bear a friend's infirmities,
But Brutus makes mine greater than they are.
"

Julius Caesar, Act IV Scene 3

"

There is a tide in the affairs of men,
Which, taken at the flood, leads on to fortune:
Omitted, all the voyage of their life
Is bound in shallows, and in miseries.
"

Julius Caesar, Act IV Scene 3

"

This was the noblest Roman of all

All the conspirators, save only he,

Did that they did in envy of great Caesar;

He only, in a general honest thought,

And common good to all, made one of them.

His life was gentle; and the elements

So mix'd in him that Nature might stand up

And say to all the world, This was a man!

"

Julius Caesar, Act V Scene 5

"

So call the field to rest: and let's away,

To part the glories of this happy day.

"

Julius Caesar, Act V Scene 5

16.

KING JOHN

- History -

A chronicle of the troublesome and often violent reign of the flawed King John.

"

And if his name be George, I'll call him Peter; For new-made honour doth forget men's names.

"

King John, Act I Scene 1

"

Sweet, sweet, sweet poison for the age's tooth.

"

King John, Act I Scene 1

"

For courage mounteth with occasion.

"

King John, Act II Scene 1

"

Thou slave, thou wretch, thou coward,
Thou little valiant, great in villany!
Thou ever strong upon the stronger side!
Thou fortune's champion, that dost never
fight
But when her humorous ladyship is by
To teach thee safety!
Thou wear a lion's hide! Doff it for shame,
And hang a calf's skin on those recreant
limbs.

"

King John, Act II Scene 1

"

Life is as tedious as a twice-told tale,
Vexing the dull ear of a drowsy man.
"

King John, Act III Scene 4

"

To gild refined gold, to paint the lily,
To throw a perfume on the violet,
To smooth the ice, or add another hue
Unto the rainbow, or with taper-light
To seek the beauteous eye of heaven to
garnish,
Is wasteful and ridiculous excess.
"

King John, Act IV Scene 2

"

Now oft the sight of means to do ill deeds
Makes deeds ill done!
"

King John, Act IV Scene 2

"

Be great in act as you have been in thought.
"

King John, Act V Scene 1

17.

KING LEAR

- Tragedy -

King Lear divides his kingdom between two of his daughters while banishing the third, who later returns with an army.

"

Nothing can come of nothing, speak again.

"

King Lear, Act I Scene

"

Mend your speech a little,
Lest you may mar your fortunes.

"

King Lear, Act I Scene 1

"

How sharper than a serpent's tooth it is,
To have a thankless child.

"

King Lear, Act I Scene 4

"

Striving to better, oft we mar what's well.

"

King Lear, Act I Scene 4

"

O, let not women's weapons, water-drops,
Stain my man's cheeks.

"

King Lear, Act II Scene 4

"

Blow, wind, and crack your cheeks! rage!
Blow!
"

King Lear, Act III Scene 2

"

Tremble, thou wretch,
That hast within thee undivulged crimes,
Unwhipped of justice.
"

King Lear, Act III Scene 2

"

I am a man
More sinned against than sinning.
"

King Lear, Act III Scene 2

"

Poor naked wretches, wheresoe'er you are,

That bide the pelting of this pitiless storm,

How shall your houseless heads, and unfed
sides,

Your looped and windowed raggedness,
defend you

From seasons such as these?

Take physic, pomp;

Expose thyself to feel what wretches feel.
"

King Lear, Act III Scene 4

"

I'll talk a word with this same learned
Theban.
"

King Lear, Act III Scene 4

"

Let me ask you one word in private.
"

King Lear, Act III Scene 4

"

The little dogs and all,
Tray, Blanch, and Sweetheart, see, they bark
at me.
"

King Lear, Act III Scene 6

"

Ay, every inch a king.
"

King Lear, Act IV Scene 6

"

Give me an ounce of civet, good apothecary,
to sweeten my imagination.
"

King Lear, Act IV Scene 6

"

Through tattered clothes small vices do
appear;
Robes and furred gowns hide all.
"

King Lear, Act IV Scene 6

"

The gods are just, and of our pleasant vices
Make instruments to plague us.
"

King Lear, Act V Scene 3

"

Her voice was ever soft,
Gentle, and low; an excellent thing in
woman.

"

King Lear, Act V Scene 3

18.

LOVE'S LABOUR'S LOST

- Comedy -

The King of Navarre and his companions attempt to avoid women to better focus on fasting and study, but this proves difficult when the Princess of France arrives.

"

Study is like the heaven's glorious sun.

"

Love's Labour's Lost, Act I Scene 1

"

Let fame, that all hunt after in their lives,
Live registered upon our brazen tombs,
And then grace us in the disgrace of death
When, spite of cormorant devouring time,
Th'endeavour of this present breath may buy
That honour which shall bate his scythe's
keen edge
And make us heirs of all eternity.
"

Love's Labour's Lost, Act I Scene 1

"

Our court shall be a little academe,
Still and contemplative in living art.
"

Love's Labour's Lost, Act I Scene 1

"

As painfully to pore upon a book
To seek the light of truth, while truth the
while
Doth falsely blind the eyesight of his look."

Love's Labour's Lost, Act I Scene 1

"

Assist me, some extemporal god of rhyme,
for I am sure I shall turn sonnet. Devise, wit:
write, pen, for I am for whole volumes in
folio.
"

Love's Labour's Lost, Act I Scene 2

"

Beauty is bought by judgement of the eye,
Not uttered by base sale of chapmen's
tongues.
"

Love's Labour's Lost, Act II Scene 1

"

Your wit's too hot, it speeds too fast, 'twill
tire.
"

Love's Labour's Lost, Act II Scene 1

"

A merrier man,
Within the limit of becoming mirth,
I never spent an hour's talk withal.
"

Love's Labour's Lost, Act II Scene 1

"

O me, with what strict patience have I sat,

To see a king transformed to a gnat!

To see great Hercules whipping a gig,

And profound Solomon tuning a jig,

And Nestor play at push-pin with the boys,

And critic Timon laugh at idle toys.

"

Love's Labour's Lost, Act IV Scene 3

"

From women's eyes this doctrine I derive:

They are the ground, the books, the
academes

From whence doth spring the true
Promethean fire.

"

Love's Labour's Lost, Act IV Scene 3

"

They have been at a great feast of languages,
and stolen the scraps.
"

Love's Labour's Lost, Act V Scene 1

"

He draweth the thread of his verbosity finer
than the staple of his argument.
"

Love's Labour's Lost, Act V Scene 1

19.
MACBETH
- Tragedy -

Macbeth kills the King of Scotland after being told by three witches that he will be crowned.

"

When shall we three meet again,
In thunder, lightning, or in rain?

"

Macbeth, Act I Scene 1

"

Fair is foul, and foul is fair.

"

Macbeth, Act I Scene 1

"

The earth hath bubbles, as the water has,
And these are of them.
"

Macbeth, Act I Scene 3

"

Two truths are told,
As happy prologues to the swelling act
Of the imperial theme.
"

Macbeth, Act I Scene 3

"

Present fears
Are less than horrible imaginings.
"

Macbeth, Act I Scene 3

"

Come what come may,
Time and the hour runs through the roughest
day.
"

Macbeth, Act I Scene 3

"

Nothing in his life
Became him like the leaving it.
"

Macbeth, Act I Scene 4

"

There's no art
To find the mind's construction in the face.
"

Macbeth, Act I Scene 4

"

Yet I do fear thy nature;
It is too full of the milk of human kindness
To catch the nearest way.
"

Macbeth, Act I Scene 5

"

Your face, my thane, is as a book, where men
May read strange matters.
"

Macbeth, Act I Scene 5

"

If it were done, when 'tis done, then 'twere
well
It were done quickly.
"

Macbeth, Act I Scene 7

"

That but this blow
Might be the be-all and the end-all here.
"

Macbeth, Act I Scene 7

"

This even-handed justice
Commends the ingredients of our poisoned
chalice
To our own lips.
"

Macbeth, Act I Scene 7

"

Besides, this Duncan

Hath borne his faculties so meek, hath been

So clear in his great office, that his virtues

Will plead like angels, trumpet-tongued,
against

The deep damnation of his taking off.

"

Macbeth, Act I Scene 7

"

I have no spur

To prick the sides of my intent, but only

Vaulting ambition, which o'erleaps itself,

And falls on the other —.

"

Macbeth, Act I Scene 7

"

I have bought
Golden opinions from all sorts of people.
"

Macbeth, Act I Scene 7

"

Letting I dare not wait upon I would,
Like the poor cat i'th'adage?
"

Macbeth, Act I Scene 7

"

I dare do all that may become a man;
Who dares do more, is none.
"

Macbeth, Act I Scene 7

"

But screw your courage to the sticking-place.
"

Macbeth, Act I Scene 7

"

Is this a dagger which I see before me,
The handle towards my hand?
"

Macbeth, Act II Scene 1

"

Thou sure and firm-set earth,
Hear not my steps, which way they walk,
for fear
The very stones prate of my whereabout.
"

Macbeth, Act II Scene 1

"

For it is a knell

That summons thee to heaven or to hell!

"

Macbeth, Act II Scene 1

"

The attempt, and not the deed,

Confound us.

"

Macbeth, Act II Scene 2

"

Sleep, that knits up the ravell'd sleave of care.

"

Macbeth, Act II Scene 2

"

Infirm of purpose!
Give me the daggers.
The sleeping and the dead
Are but as pictures; 'tis the eye of childhood
That fears a painted devil.
"

Macbeth, Act II Scene 2

"

The wine of life is drawn, and the mere lees
Is left this vault to brag of.
"

Macbeth, Act II Scene 3

"

A falcon, towering in her pride of place,
Was by a mousing owl hawked at, and killed.
"

Macbeth, Act II Scene 4

"

Upon my head they placed a fruitless crown,
And put a barren scepter in my gripe,
Thence to be wrenched with an unlineal hand,
No son of mine succeeding.
"

Macbeth, Act III Scene 1

"

Mr: We are men, my liege.
Mc: Ay, in the catalogue ye go for men.
"

Macbeth, Act III Scene 1

"

We have scotched the snake, not killed it.
"

Macbeth, Act III Scene 2

"

Duncan is in his grave!
After life's fitful fever he sleeps well.
"

Macbeth, Act III Scene 2

"

But now, I am cabined, cribbed, confined
bound in
To saucy doubts and fears.
"

Macbeth, Act III Scene 4

"

Now good digestion wait on appetite,
And health on both!
"

Macbeth, Act III Scene 4

"

Thou canst not say, I did it: never shake
Thy gory locks at me.
"

Macbeth, Act III Scene 4

"

Thou hast no speculation in those eyes
Which thou dost glare with!
"

Macbeth, Act III Scene 4

"

What man dare, I dare.

"

Macbeth, Act III Scene 4

"

Take any shape but that, and my firm nerves
Shall never tremble.

"

Macbeth, Act III Scene 4

"

Stand not upon the order of your going,
But go at once.

"

Macbeth, Act III Scene 4

"

Can such things be,
And overcome us like a summer's cloud,
Without our special wonder?
"

Macbeth, Act III Scene 4

"

Black spirits and white,
Red spirits and gray,
Mingle, mingle, mingle,
You that mingle may.
"

Macbeth, Act IV Scene 1

"

By the pricking of my thumbs,
Something wicked this way comes.
"

Macbeth, Act IV Scene 1

"

A deed without a name.

"

Macbeth, Act IV Scene 1

"

I'll make assurance double sure,
And take a bond of fate.

"

Macbeth, Act IV Scene 1

"

Show his eyes, and grieve his heart!
Come like shadows, so depart.

"

Macbeth, Act IV Scene 1

"

What! will the line stretch out to the crack of
doom?
"

Macbeth, Act IV Scene 1

"

The flighty purpose never is o'ertook,
Unless the deed go with it.
"

Macbeth, Act IV Scene 1

"

What, all my pretty chickens, and their dam,
At one fell swoop?
"

Macbeth, Act IV Scene 3

"

I cannot but remember such things were,

That were most precious to me.

"

Macbeth, Act IV Scene 3

"

O, I could play the woman with mine eyes,

And braggart with my tongue!

"

Macbeth, Act IV Scene 3

"

My way of life

Is fallen into the sear, the yellow leaf;

And that which should accompany old age,

As honor, love, obedience, troops of friends,

I must not look to have; but, in their stead,

Curses, not loud, but deep, mouth-honor,
breath,

Which the poor heart would fain deny, but
dare not.

"

Macbeth, Act V Scene 3

"

Not so sick, my lord,

As she is troubled with thick-coming fancies,

That keep her from her rest.

"

Macbeth, Act V Scene 3

"

Canst thou not minister to a mind diseased;
Pluck from the memory a rooted sorrow;
Raze out the written troubles of the brain;
And, with some sweet oblivious antidote,
Cleanse the stuffed bosom of that perilous
stuff
Which weighs upon the heart?
"

Macbeth, Act V Scene 3

"

Throw physic to the dogs: I'll none of it.
"

Macbeth, Act V Scene 3

"

I would applaud thee to the very echo,
That should applaud again.
"

Macbeth, Act V Scene 3

"

Hang out our banners on the outward walls;
The cry is still, They come.
"

Macbeth, Act V Scene 5

"

To-morrow, and to-morrow, and to-morrow,
Creeps in this petty pace from day to day,
To the last syllable of recorded time;
And all our yesterdays have lighted fools
The way to dusty death. Out, out, brief
candle!
Life's but a walking shadow; a poor player,
That struts and frets his hour upon the stage,
And then is heard no more; it is a tale
Told by an idiot, full of sound and fury,
Signifying nothing.
"

Macbeth, Act V Scene 5

"

Blow, wind! come, wrack!
At least we'll die with harness on our back.
"

Macbeth, Act V Scene 5

"

I bear a charmed life.

"

Macbeth, Act V Scene 7

"

That keep the word of promise to our ear,
And break it to our hope.

"

Macbeth, Act V Scene 7

"

Lay on, Macduff;
And damned be him that first cries, Hold,
enough!

"

Macbeth, Act V Scene 7

20.

MEASURE FOR MEASURE

- Comedy -

The Duke of Vienna steps away from public life, allowing his deputy Angelo to take advantage of the situation.

"

Spirits are not finely touch'd,
But to fine issues, nor Nature never lends
The smallest scruple of her excellence,
But, like a thrifty goddess, she determines
Herself the glory of a creditor,
Both thanks and use.

"

Measure for Measure, Act I Scene 1

"

Our doubts are traitors,
And make us lose the good we oft might win,
By fearing to attempt.
"

Measure for Measure, Act I Scene 5

"

Some rise by sin, and some by virtue fall.
"

Measure for Measure, Act II Scene 1

"

Condemn the fault, and not the actor of it?
"

Measure for Measure, Act II Scene 2

"

O, it is excellent
To have a giant's strength; but it is tyrannous
To use it like a giant.
"

Measure for Measure, Act II Scene 2

"

But man, proud man!
Drest in a little brief authority,
Plays such fantastic tricks before high
Heaven
As make the angels weep.
"

Measure for Measure, Act II Scene 2

"

The miserable have no other medicine,
But only hope.

"

Measure for Measure, Act III Scene 1

"

The sense of death is most in apprehension;
And the poor beetle that we tread upon
In corporal sufferance finds a pang as great
As when a giant dies.

"

Measure for Measure, Act III Scene 1

"

Ay, but to die, and go we know not where;
To lie in cold obstruction, and to rot.

"

Measure for Measure, Act III Scene 1

"

Take, O take those lips away,
That so sweetly were forsworn;
And those eyes, the break of day,
Lights that do mislead the morn;
But my kisses bring again,
Seals of love, but sealed in vain.

"

Measure for Measure, Act IV Scene 1

"

Truth is truth
To the end of reckoning.

"

Measure for Measure, Act V Scene 1

"

What's mine is yours and what is yours is mine.

"

Measure for Measure, Act V Scene 1

21.

THE MERCHANT OF VENICE

- Comedy -

A moneylender seeks revenge against a merchant who has defaulted on a loan.

"

I hold the world but as the world, Gratiano;
A stage, where every man must play a part,
And mine a sad one.

"

The Merchant of Venice, Act I Scene 1

"

Why should a man, whose blood is warm within,
Sit like his grandsire cut in alabaster?

"

The Merchant of Venice, Act I Scene 1

"

I am Sir Oracle,

And when I ope my lips, let no dog bark!

"

The Merchant of Venice, Act I Scene 1

"

Gratiano speaks an infinite deal of nothing;

more than any man in all

Venice. His reasons are as two grains of

wheat hid in two bushels of chaff: you shall

seek all day ere you find them: and, when

you have them, they are not worth the

search.

"

The Merchant of Venice, Act I Scene 1

"

God made him, and therefore let him pass for
a man.

"

The Merchant of Venice, Act I Scene 2

"

I will buy with you, sell with you, talk with
you, walk with you, and so following, but I
will not eat with you, drink with you, nor
pray with you. What news on the Rialto?

"

The Merchant of Venice, Act I Scene 3

"

Even there, where merchants most do
congregate.

"

The Merchant of Venice, Act I Scene 3

"

The devil can cite Scripture for his purpose.
"

The Merchant of Venice, Act I Scene 3

"

Sufferance is the badge of all our tribe.
"

The Merchant of Venice, Act I Scene 3

"

Many a time, and oft, the Rialto, have you rated me.
"

The Merchant of Venice, Act I Scene 3

"

It is a wise father that knows his own child.
"

The Merchant of Venice, Act II Scene 1

"

But love is blind, and lovers cannot see
The pretty follies that themselves commit.
"

The Merchant of Venice, Act II Scene 6

"

All things that are,
Are with more spirits chased than enjoyed.
"

The Merchant of Venice, Act II Scene 6

"

All that glisters is not gold.
"

The Merchant of Venice, Act II Scene 7

"

I am a Jew: hath not a Jew eyes? hath not a
Jew hands, organs, dimensions, senses,
affections, passions?
"

The Merchant of Venice, Act III Scene 1

"

Thus when I shun Scylla, your father, I fall
into Charybdis, your mother.
"

The Merchant of Venice, Act III Scene 5

"

What! wouldst thou have a serpent sting thee
twice?
"

The Merchant of Venice, Act IV Scene 1

"

The quality of mercy is not strained;
It droppeth, as the gentle rain from heaven
Upon the place beneath: it is twice blessed;
It blesseth him that gives, and him that takes
"

The Merchant of Venice, Act IV Scene 1

"

A Daniel come to judgment.
"

The Merchant of Venice, Act IV Scene 1

"

Is it so nominated in the bond.
"

The Merchant of Venice, Act IV Scene 1

"

I cannot find it; 'tis not in the bond.

"

The Merchant of Venice, Act IV Scene 1

"

I have thee on the hip.

"

The Merchant of Venice, Act IV Scene 1

"

I thank thee, Jew, for teaching me that word.

"

The Merchant of Venice, Act IV Scene 1

"

How sweet the moonlight sleeps upon this bank.

"

The Merchant of Venice, Act V Scene 1

"

I am never merry when I hear sweet music.

"

The Merchant of Venice, Act V Scene 1

"

The man that hath no music in himself,
Nor is not moved with concord of sweet
sounds,
Is fit for treasons, stratagems, and spoils.

"

The Merchant of Venice, Act V Scene 1

"

How far that little candle throws his beams!
So shines a good deed in a naughty world.

"

The Merchant of Venice, Act V Scene 1

"

This night, methinks, is but the daylight sick.

"

The Merchant of Venice, Act V Scene 1

"

Fair ladies, you drop manna in the way
Of starved people.

"

The Merchant of Venice, Act V Scene 1

22.

THE MERRY WIVES OF WINDSOR

- Comedy -

Falstaff cheekily sends two identical letters of love to the wives of wealthy merchants and is soon found out.

"

All his successors, gone before him, have done't; and all his ancestors, that come after him, may.

"

The Merry Wives of Windsor, Act I Scene 1

"

Thou art the Mars of malcontents.

"

The Merry Wives of Windsor, Act I Scene 3

"

Here will be an old abusing of God's patience
and the King's English.
"

The Merry Wives of Windsor, Act I Scene 4

"

I love not the humour of bread and cheese.
"

The Merry Wives of Windsor, Act II Scene 1

"

Why, then the world's mine oyster, which I
with sword will open.
"

The Merry Wives of Windsor, Act II Scene 2

"

Marry, this is the short and the long of it.
"

The Merry Wives of Windsor, Act II Scene 2

"

Setting the attractions of my good parts aside,
I have no other charms."

The Merry Wives of Windsor, Act II Scene 2

"

Like a fair house built on another man's
ground.
"

The Merry Wives of Windsor, Act II Scene 2

"

Better three hours too soon than a minute too late.

"

The Merry Wives of Windsor, Act II Scene 2

"

A man of my kidney.

"

The Merry Wives of Windsor, Act III Scene 5

"

Why, woman, your husband is in his old lines again: he so takes on yonder with my husband, so rails against all married mankind, so curses all Eve's daughters of what complexion soever.

"

The Merry Wives of Windsor, Act IV Scene 2

"

Wives may be merry, and yet honest too.

"

The Merry Wives of Windsor, Act IV Scene 2

"

I hope good luck lies in odd numbers.

"

The Merry Wives of Windsor, Act V Scene 1

"

They say, there is divinity in odd numbers,
either in nativity, chance, or death.
"

The Merry Wives of Windsor, Act V Scene 1

"

O powerful Love, that in some respects
makes a beast a man, in some other a man a
beast.
"

The Merry Wives of Windsor, Act V Scene 5

"

I think the devil will not have me damned,
lest the oil that's in me should set hell on fire.
"

The Merry Wives of Windsor, Act V Scene 5

"

In love the heavens themselves do guide the state.
Money buys lands, and wives are sold by fate."

The Merry Wives of Windsor, Act V Scene 5

23.

A MIDSUMMER NIGHT'S DREAM

- Comedy -

Puck, a mischievous fairy, causes misunderstandings when two couples enter a forest.

"

The course of true love never did run smooth.

"

A Midsummer Night's Dream, Act I Scene 1

"

Love looks not with the eyes, but with the mind, And therefore is winged Cupid painted blind.

"

A Midsummer Night's Dream, Act I Scene 1

"

I must go seek some dewdrops here,
And hang a pearl in every cowslip's ear.

"

A Midsummer Night's Dream, Act II Scene 1

"

Ill met by moonlight, proud Titania.

"

A Midsummer Night's Dream, Act II Scene 1

"

I know a bank where the wild thyme blows,
Where oxlips and the nodding violet grows,
Quite over-canopied with luscious woodbine,
With sweet musk-roses and with eglantine:
There sleeps Titania sometime of the night,
Lulled in these flowers with dances and
delight.
"

A Midsummer Night's Dream, Act II Scene 1

"

Bless thee, Bottom! Bless thee!
Thou art translated.
"

A Midsummer Night's Dream, Act III Scene 1

"

What angel wakes me from my flow'ry bed?

"

A Midsummer Night's Dream, Act III Scene 1

"

To say the truth, reason and love keep little company together nowadays.

"

A Midsummer Night's Dream, Act III Scene 1

"

O, when she's angry, she is keen and shrewd.
She was a vixen when she went to school,
And though she be but little, she is fierce.

"

A Midsummer Night's Dream, Act III Scene 2

"
Cupid is a knavish lad, Thus to make poor females mad.
"

A Midsummer Night's Dream, Act III Scene 2

"
Jack shall have Jill,
Nought shall go ill,
The man shall have his mare again, and all shall be well.
"

A Midsummer Night's Dream, Act III Scene 2

"
Methought I was enamoured of an ass.
"

A Midsummer Night's Dream, Act IV Scene 1

"

I have had a most rare vision. I had a dream, past the wit of man to say what dream it was… The eye of man hath not heard, the ear of man hath not seen, man's hand is not able to taste, his tongue to conceive, nor his heart to report, what my dream was.

"

A Midsummer Night's Dream, Act IV Scene 1

"

Not a mouse
Shall disturb this hallowed house.
I am sent with broom before,
To sweep the dust behind the door.

"

A Midsummer Night's Dream, Act V Scene 1

"

If we shadows have offended,
Think but this, and all is mended,
That you have but slumbered here
While these visions did appear.
And this weak and idle theme,
No more yielding, but a dream,
Gentles, do not reprehend;
If you pardon, we will mend.
And, as I am an honest Puck,
If we have unearned luck,
Now to 'scape the serpent's tongue,
We will make amends ere long:
Else the Puck a liar call.
So good night unto you all.
Give me your hands, if we be friends,
And Robin shall restore amends.

"

A Midsummer Night's Dream, Act V Scene 1

24.

MUCH ADO ABOUT NOTHING

- Comedy -

Two love stories are intertwined as Don Pedro, the Prince of Aragon, and his followers visit the estate of Leonato, the Governor of Messina.

"

There's a skirmish of wit between them.

"

Much Ado About Nothing, Act I Scene 1

"

In time the savage bull doth bear the yoke.

"

Much Ado About Nothing, Act I Scene 1

"

He that hath a beard is more than a youth,
and he that hath no beard is less than a man:
and he that is more than a youth is not for
me, and he that is less than a man, I am not
for him.

"

Much Ado About Nothing, Act II Scene 1

"

As merry as the day is long.

"

Much Ado About Nothing, Act II Scene 1

"

Speak low if you speak love.

"

Much Ado About Nothing, Act II Scene 1

"

Friendship is constant in all other things,
Save in the office and affairs of love.
"

Much Ado About Nothing, Act II Scene 1

"

She speaks poniards, and every word stabs.
"

Much Ado About Nothing, Act II Scene 1

"

I will not be sworn, but love may transform
me to an oyster."

Much Ado About Nothing, Act II Scene 3

"
When I said I would die a bachelor, I did not think I should live till I were married.
"

Much Ado About Nothing, Act II Scene 3

"
Some Cupid kills with arrows, some with traps.
"

Much Ado About Nothing, Act III Scene 1

"
Everyone cannot master a grief but he that has it.
"

Much Ado About Nothing, Act III Scene 2

"

Are you good men and true?

"

Much Ado About Nothing, Act III Scene 3

"

I love you with so much of my heart that none is left to protest.

"

Much Ado About Nothing, Act IV Scene 1

"

For there was never yet philosopher That could endure the toothache patiently.

"

Much Ado About Nothing, Act V Scene 1

"

In a false quarrel there is no true valour.

"

Much Ado About Nothing, Act V Scene 1

"

Thou and I are too wise to woo peaceably.

"

Much Ado About Nothing, Act V Scene 2

"

Peace! I will stop your mouth.

"

Much Ado About Nothing, Act V Scene 4

25.

OTHELLO

- Tragedy -

Othello is manipulated by Iago into thinking his wife Desdemona is unfaithful.

"

But I will wear my heart upon my sleeve For daws to peck at.

"

Othello, Act I Scene 1

"

Most potent, grave, and reverend signiors,
My very noble and approved good masters,
That I have ta'en away this old man's
daughter,
It is most true; true, I have married her:
The very head and front of my offending
Hath this extent, no more. Rude am I in my
speech,
And little bless'd with the soft phrase of
peace:
For since these arms of mine had seven years'
pith,
Till now some nine moons wasted, they have
used
Their dearest action in the tented field,
And little of this great world can I speak,
More than pertains to feats of broil and battle,
And therefore little shall I grace my cause
In speaking for myself. Yet, by your gracious
patience,

I will a round unvarnish'd tale deliver

Of my whole course of love; what drugs,

what charms,

What conjuration and what mighty magic,

For such proceeding I am charged withal,

I won his daughter.

"

Othello, Act I Scene 3

"

Wherein I spoke of most disastrous chances,

Of moving accidents, by flood and field;

Of hair-breadth 'scapes i' the imminent

deadly breach.

"

Othello, Act I Scene 3

"

My story being done

She gave me for my pains a world of signs:

She swore, In faith, 'twas strange, 'twas passing; strange; 'Twas pitiful, 'twas wondrous pitiful: She wished she had not heard it; yet she wished
That Heaven had made her such a man.
"

Othello, Act I Scene 3

"

Upon this hint I spake.
"

Othello, Act I Scene 3

"

I do perceive hero a divided duty.
"

Othello, Act I Scene 3

"

If after every tempest come such calms,
May the winds blow till they have waken'd
death!
"

Othello, Act II Scene 1

"

For I am nothing, if not critical.
"

Othello, Act II Scene 1

"

Iago. To suckle fools, and chronicle small
beer.
Des. O most lame and impotent conclusion!
"

Othello, Act II Scene 1

"

Silence that dreadful bell; it frights the isle
From her propriety.
"

Othello, Act II Scene 3

"

O thou invisible spirit of wine, if thou hast no
name to be known by, let us call thee devil!
"

Othello, Act II Scene 3

"

O that men should put an enemy in their
mouths, to steal away their brains!
"

Othello, Act II Scene 3

"

Perdition catch my soul,
But I do love thee! and when I love thee not,
Chaos is come again.
"

Othello, Act III Scene 3

"

Good name, in man and woman, dear my lord,

Is the immediate jewel of their souls.

Who steals my purse, steals trash; 'tis something, nothing;

'Twas mine, 'tis his, and has been slave to thousands;

But he that filches from me my good name

Robs roe of that which not enriches him,

And makes me poor indeed.

"

Othello, Act III Scene 3

"

O, beware, my lord, of jealousy;
It is the green-eyed monster,
which doth make
The meat it feeds on.
"

Othello, Act III Scene 3

"

Trifles, light as air,
Are, to the jealous, confirmations strong
As proofs of holy writ.
"

Othello, Act III Scene 3

"

Not poppy, nor mandragora,
Nor all the drowsy sirups of the world,
Shall ever medicine thee to that sweet sleep
Which thou ow'dst yesterday.

"

Othello, Act III Scene 3

"

He that is robbed, not wanting what is stolen,
Let him not know it, and he's not robbed at
all.

"

Othello, Act III Scene 3

"

O, now, forever,
Farewell the tranquil mind! farewell content!
Farewell the plumed troop, and the big wars,
That make ambition virtue! O farewell!
Farewell the neighing steed, and the shrill
trump,
The spirit-stirring drum, the ear-piercing fife,
Othello's occupation's gone!
"

Othello, Act III Scene 3

"

Be sure of it; give me the ocular proof:
Or by the worth of man's eternal soul,
Thou hadst been better have been born a dog
Than answer my waked wrath!
"

Othello, Act III Scene 3

"

But this denoted a foregone conclusion:
'Tis a shrewd doubt, though it be but a
dream.
"

Othello, Act III Scene 3

"

So, so, so, so: they laugh that win.
"

Othello, Act IV Scene 1

"

Steeped me in poverty to the very lips.
"

Othello, Act IV Scene 2

"

But, alas! to make me
A fixed figure, for the time of scorn
To point his slow, unmovin finger at.
"

Othello, Act IV Scene 2

"

And put in every honest hand a whip,
To lash the rascal naked through the world.
"

Othello, Act IV Scene 2

"

'Tis neither here nor there.
"

Othello, Act IV Scene 3

"

He hath a daily beauty in his life.
"

Othello, Act V Scene 1

"

I have done the state some service, and they know it.
"

Othello, Act V Scene 2

"

Speak of me as I am; nothing extenuate,

Nor set down aught in malice.

Then must you speak.

Of one that loved not wisely, but too well.

Of one, whose hand,

Like the base Júdean, threw a pearl away,

Richer than all his tribe.

Albeit unused to the melting mood.

"

Othello, Act V Scene 2

26.

PERICLES

- Comedy -

Pericles embarks on a journey involving jousting, shipwrecks and a family reunion.

"

To sing a song that old was sung
From ashes ancient Gower is come.

"

Pericles, Prologue

"

For death remembered should be like a
mirror
Who tells us life's but breath, to trust it error.

"

Pericles, Act I Scene 1

"

Few love to hear the sins they love to act.
"

Pericles, Act I Scene 1

"

Murder's as near to lust as flame to smoke.
"

Pericles, Act I Scene 1

"

Which care of them, not pity of myself,
Who am no more but as the tops of trees.
Which fence the roots they grow by and
defend them,
Makes both my body pine and soul to
languish.
"

Pericles, Act I Scene 2

"

'Tis time to fear when tyrants seems to kiss.

"

Pericles, Act I Scene 2

"

My Dionzya, shall we rest us here
And by relating tales of others' griefs
See if 'twill teach us to forget our own?

"

Pericles, Act I Scene 4

"

Who makes the fairest show means most
deceit.

"

Pericles, Act I Scene 4

"

Why, as men do a-land; the great ones eat up
the little ones.
"

Pericles, Act II Scene 1

"

Opinion's but a fool that makes us scan
The outward habit for the inward man.
"

Pericles, Act II Scene 2

"

The diamonds of a most praised water
Doth appear, to make the world twice rich.
"

Pericles, Act III Scene 2

"

That she would make a puritan of the devil if
he should cheapen a kiss of her.

"

Pericles, Act IV Scene 5

"

O, come, be buried
A second time within these arms.

"

Pericles, Act V Scene 3

27.

RICHARD II

- History -

Richard II follows wasteful and unwise habits as they lead him in the direction of his downfall.

"

Forget, forgive, conclude and be agreed:
Our doctors say this is no time to bleed.

"

Richard II, Act I Scene 1

"

We were not born to sue, but to command.

"

Richard II, Act I Scene 1

"

R: Why uncle, thou hast many years to live.

G: But not a minute, king, that thou canst give.

"

Richard II, Act I Scene 3

"

This royal throne of kings, this sceptred isle,

This earth of majesty, this seat of Mars.

Richard II, Act II Scene 1

"

This blessed plot, this earth, this realm, this England.

"

Richard II, Act II Scene 1

"

Landlord of England art thou and not king.
"

Richard II, Act II Scene 1

"

The ripest fruit first falls.
"

Richard II, Act II Scene 1

"

Come, lords, away.
To fight with Glendower and his complices;
A while to work and after holiday.
"

Richard II, Act III Scene 1

"

Not all the water in the rough rude sea
Can wash the balm from an anointed king.
"

Richard II, Act III Scene 2

"

For heaven's sake let us sit upon the ground
And tell sad stories of the death of kings.
"

Richard II, Act III Scene 2

"

See, see, King Richard doth himself appear,
As doth the blushing discontented sun
From out the fiery portal of the east.

Richard II, Act III Scene 2

"

What must the king do now? Must he
submit?
The King shall do it.
"

Richard II, Act III Scene 3

"

Great Duke of Lancaster, I come to thee
From plume-plucked Richard, who with
willing soul
Adopts thee heir, and his high sceptre yields
To the possession of thy royal hand.
"

Richard II, Act IV Scene 1

"

With mine own tears I wash away my balm,
With mine own hands I give away my crown.
"

Richard II, Act IV Scene 1

"

The shadow of your sorrow hath destroyed
The shadow of your face.
"

Richard II, Act IV Scene 1

"

Doubly divorced? Bad men, ye violate
A twofold marriage, 'twixt my crown and me
And then betwixt me and my married wife.
"

Richard II, Act V Scene 1

"

I wasted time, and now doth time waste me.
"

Richard II, Act V Scene 5

"

For now the devil that told me I did well
Says that this deed is chronicled in hell.
This dead king to the living king I'll bear. –
Take hence the rest, and give them burial
here.
"

Richard II, Act V Scene 5

"

Though I did wish him dead,
I hate the murd'rer, love him murdered.
"

Richard II, Act V Scene 5

"

I'll make a voyage to the Holy Land
To wash this blood off from my guilty hand.
"

Richard II, Act V Scene 6

28.

RICHARD III

- History -

Richard of Gloucester uses manipulation and murder in his rise to be crowned as king.

"

Now is the winter of our discontent
Made glorious summer by this sun of York;
And all the clouds that lowered upon our
house,
In the deep bosom of the ocean buried.

"

Richard III, Act I Scene 1

"

Cheated of feature by dissembling nature,
Deformed, unfinished, Bent before my time
Into this breathing world, scarce half made
up.
"

Richard III, Act I Scene 1

Why I, in this weak, piping time of peace,
Have no delight to pass away the time.
"

Richard III, Act I Scene 1

"

To leave this keen encounter of our wits.
"

Richard III, Act I Scene 2

"

Was ever woman in this humor wooed?
Was ever woman in this humor won?
"

Richard III, Act I Scene 2

"

O, I have passed a miserable night,
So full of fearful dreams, of ugly sights,
That, as I am a Christian faithful man,
I would not spend another such a night,
Though 'twere to buy a world of happy days.
"

Richard III, Act I Scene 4

"

Thou troublest me; I am not in the vein.
"

Richard III, Act IV Scene 2

"

Let not the heavens hear these telltale women
Hail on the Lord's anointed.

"

Richard III, Act IV Scene 4

"

An honest tale speeds best, being plainly
told.

"

Richard III, Act IV Scene 4

"

Thus far into the bowels of the land
Have we marched on without impediment.

"

Richard III, Act V Scene 2

"

True hope is swift,
and flies with swallow's wings,
Kings it makes gods,
and meaner creatures kings.
"

Richard III, Act V Scene 2

"

The king's name is a tower of strength.
"

Richard III, Act V Scene 3

"

I have set my life upon a cast,
And I will stand the hazard of the die.
"

Richard III, Act V Scene 4

"

A horse! A horse! My kingdom for a horse!

"

Richard III, Act V Scene 4

"

We will unite the white rose and the red: —
Smile heaven upon this fair conjunction,
That long have frown'd upon their emnity!

"

Richard III, Act V Scene 5

29.

ROMEO AND JULIET

- Tragedy -

Romeo and Juliet fall in love despite the ongoing and often violent feud between their families.

"

A pair of star-crossed lovers take their life.

"

Romeo and Juliet, Prologue

"

A: Do you bite your thumb at us, sir?
S: I do bite my thumb, sir.

"

Romeo and Juliet, Act I Scene 1

"

The weakest goes to the wall.
"

Romeo and Juliet, Act I Scene 1

"

Put up your swords;
you know not what you do.
"

Romeo and Juliet, Act I Scene 1

"

One fire burns out another's burning.
One pain is lessened by another's anguish.
"

Romeo and Juliet, Act I Scene 2

"

Too early seen unknown,
and known too late.
"

Romeo and Juliet, Act I Scene 5

"

But, soft, what light through yonder window
breaks?
It is the east, and Juliet is the sun.
"

Romeo and Juliet, Act II Scene 1

"

That which we call a rose
By any other word would smell as sweet.
"

Romeo and Juliet, Act II Scene 1

"

Parting is such sweet sorrow.

"

Romeo and Juliet, Act II Scene 1

"

He jests at scars, that never felt a wound.

"

Romeo and Juliet, Act II Scene 2

"

See, how she leans her cheek upon her hand!
O that I were a glove upon that hand,
That I might touch that cheek!

"

Romeo and Juliet, Act II Scene 2

"

O Romeo, Romeo! Wherefore art thou
Romeo?
"

Romeo and Juliet, Act II Scene 2

"

What's in a name? That which we call a rose
By any other name would smell as sweet.
"

Romeo and Juliet, Act II Scene 2

"

Alack! There lies more peril in thine eye,
Than twenty of their swords.
"

Romeo and Juliet, Act II Scene 2

"

At lover's perjuries,
They say, Jove laughs.
"

Romeo and Juliet, Act II Scene 2

"

O swear not by the moon, the inconstant
moon,
That monthly changes in her circled orb,
Lest that thy love prove likewise variable.
"

Romeo and Juliet, Act II Scene 2

"

Good-night, good-night! parting is such
sweet sorrow,
That I shall say good-night till it be morrow.
"

Romeo and Juliet, Act II Scene 2

"

Thy old groans ring yet in my ancient ears.
"

Romeo and Juliet, Act II Scene 3

"

Stabbed with a white wench's black eye.
"

Romeo and Juliet, Act II Scene 4

"

I am the very pink of courtesy.
"

Romeo and Juliet, Act II Scene 4

"

My man's as true as steel.
"

Romeo and Juliet, Act II Scene 4

"

These violent delights have violent ends.
"

Romeo and Juliet, Act II Scene 5

"

Here comes the lady;—O, so light a foot
Will ne'er wear out the everlasting flint.
"

Romeo and Juliet, Act II Scene 6

"

A plague o' both your houses!
"

Romeo and Juliet, Act III Scene 1

"

Mercy but murders, pardoning those that kill.

"

Romeo and Juliet, Act III Scene 1

"

Adversity's sweet milk, philosophy.

"

Romeo and Juliet, Act III Scene 3

"

O deadly sin! O rude unthankfulness!

"

Romeo and Juliet, Act III Scene 3

"

Hang thee, young baggage, disobedient wretch!
I tell thee what: get thee to church o'Thursday,
Or never after look me in the face.
"

Romeo and Juliet, Act III Scene 5

"

Night's candles are burnt out, and jocund day
Stands tiptoe on the misty mountain-tops.
"

Romeo and Juliet, Act III Scene 5

"

Not stopping o'er the bounds of modesty.
"

Romeo and Juliet, Act IV Scene 2

"

My bosom's lord sits lightly in his throne.
"

Romeo and Juliet, Act V Scene 1

"

A beggarly account of empty boxes.
"

Romeo and Juliet, Act V Scene 1

"

My poverty, but not my will, consents.
"

Romeo and Juliet, Act V Scene 1

"

Beauty's ensign yet
Is crimson in thy lips, and in thy cheeks,
And death's pale flag is not advanced there.
"

Romeo and Juliet, Act V Scene 3

"

Eyes, look your last!
Arms, take your last embrace!
"

Romeo and Juliet, Act V Scene 3

"

O true apothecary,
Thy drugs are quick. Thus with a kiss I die.
"

Romeo and Juliet, Act V Scene 3

"

O happy dagger,
This is thy sheath: there rust, and let me die.
"

Romeo and Juliet, Act V Scene 3

"

For never was a story of more woe
Than this of Juliet and her Romeo.
"

Romeo and Juliet, Act V Scene 3

30.
THE TAMING OF THE SHREW

- Comedy -

Lucentio is in love with Bianca but cannot court her until her older sister marries.

"

No profit grows where is no pleasure ta'en: In brief, sir, study what you most affect.

"

The Taming of the Shrew, Act I Scene 1

"

There's small choice in rotten apples.

"

The Taming of the Shrew, Act I Scene 1

"

Say that she rail, why then I'll tell her plain
She sings as sweetly as a nightingale:
Say that she frown, I'll say she looks as clear
As morning roses newly washed with dew:
Say she be mute and will not speak a word,
Then I'll commend her volubility,
And say she uttereth piercing eloquence:
If she do bid me pack, I'll give her thanks,
As though she bid me stay by her a week:
If she deny to wed, I'll crave the day
When I shall ask the banns and when be
married.

"

The Taming of the Shrew, Act II Scene 1

"

You lie, in faith, for you are called plain Kate,
And bonny Kate and sometimes Kate the
curst,
But Kate, the prettiest Kate in Christendom,
Kate of Kate Hall, my super-dainty Kate.

"

The Taming of the Shrew, Act II Scene 1

"

If I be waspish, best beware my sting.

The Taming of the Shrew, Act II Scene 1

"

"

Old fashions please me best. I am not so nice
To change true rules for old inventions.

"

The Taming of the Shrew, Act III Scene 1

"

And thereby hangs a tale.
"

The Taming of the Shrew, Act IV Scene 1

"

Forward, I pray, since we have come so far,
And be it moon, or sun, or what you please.
And if you please to call it a rush-candle,
Henceforth I vow it shall be so for me.
"

The Taming of the Shrew, Act IV Scene 5

"

Fie, fie! Unknit that threat'ning unkind brow,
And dart not scornful glances from those
eyes,
To wound thy lord, thy king, thy governor.
"

The Taming of the Shrew, Act V Scene 1

"

Why are our bodies soft and weak and smooth,

Unapt to toil and trouble in the world,

But that our soft conditions and our hearts

Should well agree with our external parts?

"

The Taming of the Shrew, Act V Scene 1

"

Why, there's a wench! Come on, and kiss me, Kate.

"

The Taming of the Shrew, Act V Scene 1

31.

THE TEMPEST

- Comedy -

The crew of a ship are left stranded on a Mediterranean island after the magical Prospero conjures a storm.

"

Now would I give a thousand furlongs of sea for an acre of barren ground.

"

The Tempest, Act I Scene 1

"

O, I have suffered
With those that I saw suffer.

"

The Tempest, Act I Scene 2

"

My library was dukedom large enough.
"

The Tempest, Act I Scene 2

"

For I am all the subjects that you have,
Which first was mine own king.
"

The Tempest, Act I Scene 2

"

Misery acquaints a man with strange
bedfellows.
"

The Tempest, Act II Scene 2

"

Hast thou not dropped from heaven?
"

The Tempest, Act II Scene 2

"

I am your wife, if you will marry me:
If not, I'll die your maid: to be your fellow
You may deny me, but I'll be your servant,
Whether you will or no.
"

The Tempest, Act III Scene 1

"

The clouds methought would open and show
riches
Ready to drop upon me, that when I waked,
I cried to dream again.
"

The Tempest, Act III Scene 2

"

Our revels now are ended. These our actors,

As I foretold you, were all spirits and

Are melted into air, into thin air;

And, like the baseless fabric of this vision,

The cloud-capp'd towers, the gorgeous palaces,

The solemn temples, the great globe itself,

Yea, all which it inherit, shall dissolve,

And, like this insubstantial pageant faded,

Leave not a rack behind. We are such stuff

As dreams are made on: and our little life

Is rounded with a sleep.

"

The Tempest, Act IV Scene 1

"

Where the bee sucks, there suck I:
In a cowslip's bell I lie:
There I couch when owls do cry.
On the bat's back I do fly
After summer merrily.
Merrily, merrily, shall I live now
Under the blossom that hangs on the bough.
"

The Tempest, Act V Scene 1

"

O, wonder!
How many goodly creatures are there here!
How beauteous mankind is! O brave new
world,
That has such people in't.
"

The Tempest, Act V Scene 1

"

As you from crimes would pardoned be,
Let your indulgence set me free.
"

The Tempest, Epilogue

32.

TIMON OF ATHENS

- Tragedy -

Timon is a wealthy and generous person who eventually runs out of money and loses all love for humanity.

"

The fire i'th' flint
Shows not till it be struck.

"

Timon of Athens, Act I Scene 1

"

I am not of that feather to shake off
My friend when he must need me.

"

Timon of Athens, Act I Scene 1

"

Here's that which is too weak to be a sinner—
Honest water—which ne'er left man i'th'mire.
"

Timon of Athens, Act I Scene 2

"

Like madness is the glory of this life.
"

Timon of Athens, Act I Scene 2

"

Men shut their doors against a setting sun.
"

Timon of Athens, Act I Scene 2

"

Their blood is caked, 'tis cold, it selfdom
flows:
'Tis lack of kindly warmth they are not kind.

"

Timon of Athens, Act II Scene 2

"

Every man has his fault, and honesty is his.

"

Timon of Athens, Act III Scene 2

"

Nothing emboldens sin so much as mercy.

"

Timon of Athens, Act III Scene 6

"

Timon will to the woods, where he shall find

Th'unkindest beast more kinder than

mankind.

The gods confound — hear me, you good

gods all —

Th'Athenians both within and out that wall,

And grant, as Timon grows, his hate may

grow

To the whole race of mankind, high and low!

Amen.

"

Timon of Athens, Act IV Scene 1

"

We have seen better days.

"

Timon of Athens, Act IV Scene 2

"

Strange, unusual blood,
When man's worst sin is he does too much
good!
"

Timon of Athens, Act IV Scene 2

"

Who seeks for better of thee, sauce his palate
With thy most operant poison!
"

Timon of Athens, Act IV Scene 3

"

What beast couldst thou be that were not
subject to a beast? And what a beast art thou
already, that see'st not thy loss in
transformation!
"

Timon of Athens, Act IV Scene 3

"

The moon's an arrant thief,
And her pale fire she snatches from the sun.
"

Timon of Athens, Act IV Scene 3

"

You are an alchemist, make gold of that.
"

Timon of Athens, Act V Scene 1

"

Here lies a wretched corpse, of wretched soul
bereft.
Seek not my name. A plague consume you
wicked caitiffs left!
Here lie I, Timon, who alive all living men
did hate:
Pass by and curse they fill, but pass and stay
not here thy gait.

"

Timon of Athens, Act V Scene 4

33.

TITUS ANDRONICUS

- Tragedy -

The prisoners of a Roman nobleman vow to take violent
revenge on him.

"

O cruel, irreligious piety!

"

Titus Andronicus, Act I Scene 1

"

Content thee, prince, I will restore to thee
The people's hearts, and wean them from
themselves.

"

Titus Andronicus, Act I Scene 1

"

And make them know what 'tis to let a queen
Kneel in the streets and beg for grace in vain.
"

Titus Andronicus, Act I Scene 1

"

She is a woman, therefore may be wooed:
She is a woman, therefore may be won:
She is Lavinia, therefore must be loved.
"

Titus Andronicus, Act II Scene 1

"

Madam, though Venus govern your desires,
Saturn is dominator over mine.
"

Titus Andronicus, Act II Scene 3

"

Vengeance is in my heart, death in my hand,
Blood and revenge are hammering in my
head.
"

Titus Andronicus, Act II Scene 3

"

The worse to her, the better loved of me.
"

Titus Andronicus, Act II Scene 3

"

Alas, a crimson river of warm blood,
Like to a bubbling fountain stirred with
wind,
Doth rise and fall between thy rosed lips,
Coming and going with thy honey breath.
"

Titus Andronicus, Act II Scene 4

"

Why, foolish Lucius, dost thou not perceive
That Rome is but a wilderness of tigers?
"

Titus Andronicus, Act III Scene 1

"

Alas, poor man!
Grief has so wrought on him,
He takes false shadows for true substances.
"

Titus Andronicus, Act III Scene 2

"

D: Villain, what hast thou done?
A: That which thou canst not undo.
"

Titus Andronicus, Act IV Scene 2

"

I have done a thousand dreadful things
As willingly as one would kill a fly,
And nothing grieves me heartily indeed
But that I cannot do ten thousand more.
"

Titus Andronicus, Act V Scene 1

"

Die, die, Lavinia, and thy shame with thee,
And with thy shame thy father's sorrow die!
"

Titus Andronicus, Act V Scene 3

"

O, let me teach you how to knit again
This scattered corn into one mutual sheaf,
These broken limbs again into one body.
"

Titus Andronicus, Act V Scene 3

34.

TROILUS AND CRESSIDA

- Tragedy -

Troilus and Cressida have their loyalty tested in the seventh year of the siege of Troy.

"

Things won are done, joy's soul lies in the doing.

"

Troilus and Cressida, Act I Scene 1

"

Her bed is India: there she lies, a pearl.

"

Troilus and Cressida, Act I Scene 1

"

A: They say he is a very man per se, and stands alone.
C: So do all men, unless they are drunk, sick, or have no legs.

"

Troilus and Cressida, Act I Scene 1

"

Things won are done, joy's soul lies in the doing.
That she beloved knows nought that knows nought this:
Men prize the thing ungained more than it is.

"

Troilus and Cressida, Act I Scene 2

"

The heavens themselves, the planets and this centre

Observe degree, priority and place,

Insisture, course, proportion, season, form,

Office and custom, in all line of order.

"

Troilus and Cressida, Act I Scene 3

"

There is seen

The baby figure of the giant mass

Of things to come at large.

"

Troilus and Cressida, Act I Scene 3

"

We turn not back the silks upon the merchant
When we have spoiled them.

"

Troilus and Cressida, Act II Scene 2

"

The common curse of mankind, folly and
ignorance, be thine in great revenue!

"

Troilus and Cressida, Act II Scene 3

"

They say all lovers swear more performance
than they are able.

"

Troilus and Cressida, Act III Scene 2

"

Time hath, my lord, a wallet at his back,

Wherein he puts alms for oblivion,

A great-sized monster of ingratitudes:

Those scraps are good deeds past; which are

devoured

As fast as they are made, forgot as soon

As done.

"

Troilus and Cressida, Act III Scene 3

"

One touch of nature makes the whole world

kin.

"

Troilus and Cressida, Act III Scene 3

"

And, like a dewdrop from the lion's mane,

Be shook to air.

"

Troilus and Cressida, Act III Scene 3

"

A plague of opinion! A man may wear it on

both sides, like a leather jerkin.

"

Troilus and Cressida, Act III Scene 3

"

Time, force and death,

Do to this body what extremity you can;

But the strong base and building of my love

Is as the very centre of the earth,

Drawing all things to it.

"

Troilus and Cressida, Act IV Scene 2

"

There's language in her eye, her cheek, her
lip;
Nay, her foot speaks, her wanton spirits look
out
At every joint and motive of her body.
"

Troilus and Cressida, Act IV Scene 5

"

The end crowns all,
And that old common arbitrator, Time,
Will one day end it.
"

Troilus and Cressida, Act IV Scene 5

35.

TWELFTH NIGHT

- Comedy -

Twins separated by shipwreck each believes the other to be drowned.

"

If music be the food of love, play on,
Give me excess of it; that, surfeiting,
The appetite may sicken, and so die.—
That strain again—it had a dying fall;
O, it came o'er my ear like the sweet south,
That breathes upon a bank of violets,
Stealing and giving odor.

"

Twelfth Night, Act I Scene 1

"

What country, friends, is this?
"

Twelfth Night, Act I Scene 2

"

But I am a great eater of beef, and I believe
that does harm to my wit.
"

Twelfth Night, Act I Scene 3

"

I am sure care's an enemy to life.
"

Twelfth Night, Act I Scene 3

"

'Tis beauty truly blent, whose red and white
Nature's own sweet and cunning hand laid
on.
"

Twelfth Night, Act I Scene 5

"

Many a good hanging prevents a bad
marriage.
"

Twelfth Night, Act I Scene 5

"

Better a witty fool than a foolish wit.
"

Twelfth Night, Act I Scene 5

"

Dost thou think, because them art virtuous,
there shall be no more cakes and ale?
"

Twelfth Night, Act II Scene 3

"

She never told her love,
But let concealment, like a worm in the bud,
Feed on her damask cheek: she pined in
thought,
And, with a green and yellow melancholy,
She sat, like Patience on a monument,
Smiling at grief.
"

Twelfth Night, Act II Scene 4

"

O, what a deal of scorn looks beautiful
In the contempt and anger of his lip!

"

Twelfth Night, Act III Scene 1

"

Love sought is good, but given unsought is
better.

"

Twelfth Night, Act III Scene 1

"

Let there be gall enough in thy ink; though
thou write with a goose-pen, no matter.

"

Twelfth Night, Act III Scene 2

"

If this were played upon a stage now, I could
condemn it as an improbable fiction.
"

Twelfth Night, Act III Scene 4

"

Prove true, imagination, O, prove true,
That I, dear brother, be now ta'en for you!
"

Twelfth Night, Act III Scene 4

"

One face, one voice, one habit, and two
persons,
A natural perspective that is and is not!
"

Twelfth Night, Act V Scene 1

"

And thus the whirligig of time brings in his revenges.

"

Twelfth Night, Act V Scene 1

"

I'll be revenged on the whole pack of you.

"

Twelfth Night, Act V Scene 1

"

Cesario, come –

For so you shall be, while you are a man.

But when in other habits you are seen,

Orsino's mistress, and his fancy's queen.

"

Twelfth Night, Act V Scene 1

36.

THE TWO GENTLEMEN OF VERONA

- Comedy -

After traveling to Milan, two best friends both fall in love with Silvia.

"

For he was more than over-shoes in love.

"

The Two Gentlemen of Verona, Act I Scene 1

"

I have no other, but a woman's reason:
I think him so because I think him so.

"

The Two Gentlemen of Verona, Act I Scene 2

"
They do not love that do not show their love.
"

The Two Gentlemen of Verona, Act I Scene 2

"
You, minion, are too saucy.
"

The Two Gentlemen of Verona, Act I Scene 2

"
O hateful hands, to tear such loving words;
Injurious wasps, to feed on such sweet honey
And kill the bees that yield it, with your
stings!
I'll kiss each several paper for amends.
"

The Two Gentlemen of Verona, Act I Scene 2

"

O, how this spring of love resembleth
The uncertain glory of an April day,
Which now shows all the beauty of the sun,
And by and by a cloud takes all away."

The Two Gentlemen of Verona, Act I Scene 3

"

I'll be as patient as a gentle stream,
And make a pastime of each weary step,
Till the last step have brought me to my love,
And there I'll rest, as after much turmoil,
A blessed soul doth in Elysium.

"

The Two Gentlemen of Verona, Act II Scene 7

"

That man that hath a tongue, I say is no man,
If with his tongue he cannot win a woman.
"

The Two Gentlemen of Verona, Act III Scene 1

"

Love is like a child
That longs for every thing that he can come
by."

The Two Gentlemen of Verona, Act III Scene 1

"

And why not death, rather than living
torment?
To die is to be banished from myself;
And Silvia is myself: banished from her,
Is self from self. A deadly banishment:
What light is light, if Silvia be not seen?
What joy is joy, if Silvia be not by?
"

The Two Gentlemen of Verona, Act III Scene 1

"

To make a virtue of necessity.
"

The Two Gentlemen of Verona, Act IV Scene 1

"

Is she not passing fair?
"

The Two Gentlemen of Verona, Act IV Scene 4

"

She dreams on him that has forgot her love,
You dote on her that cares not for your love.
'Tis pity love should be so contrary:
And thinking on it makes me cry 'Alas'.

"

The Two Gentlemen of Verona, Act IV Scene 4

"

O heaven, were man
But constant, he were perfect.

"

The Two Gentlemen of Verona, Act V Scene 4

37.

THE TWO NOBLE KINSMEN

- Comedy -

Two imprisoned cousins, Palamon and Arcite, do their all to woo Emilia.

"

Come all sad and solemn shows,
That are quick-eyed Pleasure's foes:
We convent naught else but woes.
We convent naught else but woes.

"

Two Noble Kinsmen, Act I Scene 5

"

This world's a city full of straying streets,
And death's the market-place where each one
meets.
"

Two Noble Kinsmen, Act I Scene 5

"

Whilst Palamon is with me, let me perish
If I think this our prison.
"

Two Noble Kinsmen, Act II Scene 2

"

It is the very emblem of a maid.

For when the west wind courts her gently,

How modestly she blows and paints the sun

With her chaste blushes. When the north

comes near her,

Rude and impatient, then, like chastity,

She locks her beauties in her bud again,

And leaves him to base briars.

"

Two Noble Kinsmen, Act II Scene 2

"

Fie, sir. You play the child extremely."

Two Noble Kinsmen, Act II Scene 2

"

Once he kissed me.
I loved my lips the better ten days after:
Would he would do so every day!
"

Two Noble Kinsmen, Act II Scene 4

"

O you heavens, dares any
So nobly bear a guilty business? None
But only Arcite: therefore none but Arcite
In this kind is so bold.
"

Two Noble Kinsmen, Act III Scene 1

"

'Tis pity love should be so tyrannous.
"

Two Noble Kinsmen, Act IV Scene 2

"

I am bride-habited,
But maiden-hearted.

"

Two Noble Kinsmen, Act V Scene 1

"

O great corrector of enormous times,
Of dusty and old titles, that heal'st with
blood
The earth when it is sick, and cur'st the world
O'th'pleurisy of people.

"

Two Noble Kinsmen, Act V Scene 1

38.

THE WINTER'S TALE

- Comedy -

Tragic events set in motion by the jealous King Leontes are balanced by fairy-tale ending.

"

I speak as my understanding instructs me
and as mine honesty puts it to utterance.
"

The Winter's Tale, Act I Scene 1

"

How say you?
My prisoner? Or my guest? by your dread
'Verily',
One of them you shall be.
"

The Winter's Tale, Act I Scene 2

"

What we changed

Was innocence for innocence. We knew not

The doctrine of ill-doing, nor dreamed

That any did."

The Winter's Tale, Act I Scene 2

"

Be plainer with me. Let me know my trespass

By its own visage; if I then deny it,

'Tis none of mine.

"

The Winter's Tale, Act I Scene 2

"

Is this nothing?

Why then the world and all that's in't is

nothing:

The covering sky is nothing, Bohemia

nothing,

My wife is nothing, nor nothing have these

nothings,

If this be nothing.

"

The Winter's Tale, Act I Scene 2

"

The silence often of pure innocence

Persuades when speaking fails.

"

The Winter's Tale, Act II Scene 2

"

It shall scarce boot me
To say 'Not guilty': mine integrity
Being counted falsehood, shall, as I express it,
Be so received. But thus: if powers divine
Behold our human actions, as they do,
I doubt not then but innocence shall make
False accusation blush and tyranny
Tremble at patience.
"

The Winter's Tale, Act III Scene 2

"

Apollo's angry, and the heavens themselves
Do strike at my injustice.
"

The Winter's Tale, Act III Scene 2

"

Exit, pursued by a bear.

"

The Winter's Tale, Act III Scene 3 Stage Direction

"

Since it is in my power
To o'erthrow law and in one self-born hour
To plant and o'erwhelm custom.

"

The Winter's Tale, Act IV Scene 1

"

A merry heart goes all the day,
Your sad tires in a mile-a.

"

The Winter's Tale, Act IV Scene 2

"

Daffodils,

That come before the swallow dares, and take

The winds of March with beauty; violets,

dim,

But sweeter than the lids of Juno's eyes,

Or Cytherea's breath.

"

The Winter's Tale, Act IV Scene 3

"

When you do dance, I wish you

A wave o' the sea, that you might ever do

Nothing but that.

"

The Winter's Tale, Act IV Scene 3

"

What a fool honesty is!

"

The Winter's Tale, Act IV Scene 4

"

Though I am not naturally honest, I am so sometimes by chance.

"

The Winter's Tale, Act IV Scene 4

"

I am ashamed. Does not the stone rebuke me For being more stone than it?

"

The Winter's Tale, Act V Scene 3

NOTABLE CHARACTERS FROM SHAKESPEARE'S PLAYS

Antonio

The Merchant of Venice

Ariel

The Tempest

Beatrice

Much Ado About Nothing

Benedick

Much Ado About Nothing

Caliban

The Tempest

Claudius

Hamlet

Cleopatra

Antony and Cleopatra

Cordelia

King Lear

Desdemona

Othello

Duncan

Macbeth

Sir John Falstaff

Henry IV Part I, Henry IV Part II, Henry V and The Merry Wives of Windsor

Friar Laurence

Romeo and Juliet

Gertrude

Hamlet

Goneril

King Lear

Prince Hal

Henry IV Part I and Henry V

Hamlet

Hamlet

Herne the Hunter

The Merry Wives of Windsor

Iago

Othello

Juliet

Romeo and Juliet

Julius Caesar
Julius Caesar

Katherine
The Taming of the Shrew

Lady Macbeth
Macbeth

Macbeth
Macbeth

Malcolm
Macbeth

Marcus Brutus
Julius Caesar

Miranda
The Tempest

Nick Bottom
A Midsummer Night's Dream

Oberon
A Midsummer Night's Dream

Ophelia
Hamlet

Orlando
As You Like It

Othello
Othello

Petruchio
The Taming of the Shrew

Pistol
Henry IV Part I, Henry IV Part II, Henry V and The Merry Wives of Windsor

Polonius
Hamlet

Portia
The Merchant of Venice

Prospero
The Tempest

Puck
A Midsummer Night's Dream

Regan
King Lear

Richard III
Henry VI Part II, Henry VI Part III and Richard III

Romeo

Romeo and Juliet

Rosalind

As You Like It

Shylock

The Merchant of Venice

Titania

A Midsummer Night's Dream

Touchstone

As You Like It

Viola

Twelfth Night

Weird Sisters

Macbeth

Printed in Great Britain
by Amazon

85961533R00190